BARIATRIC COOKBOOK (THE ULTIMATE MEGA GUIDE)

The ultimate Bariatric guide composed by two books: Bariatric cookbook + Bariatric meal prep

CASEY CALDWELL

Copyright Casey Caldwell © 2023,

All Rights Reserved.

Table of contents

Introduction 4
Chapter 1: Post-Surgery 9
Chapter 2: Dietary 49
Chapter 3: Breakfast 84
Chapter 4: SidesMeals 119
Chapter 5: Dinner 159
Chapter 6: Desserts 194
Conclusion 223
Introduction 226
Chapter 1: What You Must Understand 231
Chapter 2: Breakfast 244
Chapter 3: Lunch 334
Chapter 4: Other Varieties 341
Chapter 5: Dinner 417
Conclusion 498

Introduction

I don't have a specific formula for success, but I will share one with you right away because it is very important. This book contains a lot of straightforward and inviting recipes that can entice you, but I want to share one with you in particular right now because it is significant. You need to have the four "ingredient abilities" that will help you achieve in order to be successful. You'll be able to reach your full potential by doing this.

Even if it's only a fresh take on an old favorite, if you're prepared to attempt something unusual, you'll be amply rewarded for your efforts. Let's assume that you are open to trying new things, even if they just involve a novel twist on a tried-and-true recipe. You should try Greek yogurt if you haven't already since you might discover that it fills your hunger more than the standard yogurt cup you've been ingesting for the past few years. Greek yogurt is a tasty dairy product. Greek yogurt often has more cream and is thicker than plain yogurt. Compared to conventional yogurt, which is thinner, Greek yogurt is creamier.

Additionally, Greek yogurt has nearly twice as much protein as normal yogurt. I can't recall if I said that. I believe I've said it before.

Many people worry that they won't be able to eat any of their favorite foods since they would have to give them up in order to reach their target weight. This is true if they want to lose weight effectively for the rest of their lives. Even if it wanted to, this could not be further from the truth. This is the furthest thing from reality that is. By making only a few minor changes to the way you regularly prepare the meals, you can incorporate the foods you already like into your long-term post-operative diet. You will therefore be able to consume nearly everything.

Despite the fact that you are aware that protein is a crucial part of the bariatric diet, you shouldn't let this deter you because there are other ways to get protein besides egg whites and poached salmon. We also promise that once you figure out how to add the required protein to a diversified diet, it won't taste like a covert operation.

Whether a difficult time lasts a few days or several weeks, your ability to bounce back and move on will determine how you'll end up in this world. It doesn't matter how long the challenging time is.

You have a strong desire to keep living life to the fullest. Focus on the present while concurrently setting goals for the near future if you don't want to be sidetracked by thoughts of the past.

There is nothing else to be said about it save that. You did an excellent job! Combine the key elements described in the sentences that follow. Your long-term goals of improving your general health and reducing your body fat percentage will be simpler to reach. It is only fair and acceptable that the opening chapter of this book focus on you and the other members of your surgical team. You must attentively cooperate with the great instruments provided by the hospital where the surgery is being performed if you want to successfully complete this complicated treatment. You can guarantee that you make the most of the support given by doing this. No matter which sort of weight-reduction surgery a person chooses, I'll go through the fundamental ideas because there isn't a one-size-fits-all strategy for weight loss. I'll go through the core ideas that everybody should be aware of, irrespective of the kind of weight-loss surgery they choose. Regardless of the kind of weight-loss surgery a person chooses, I will go over the fundamental ideas that apply to everyone and explain why they are so crucial. To find out if you need to follow any special dietary restrictions due to you or the sort of operation you're having, make sure to consult a trained nutritionist.

Chapter One

Post-Surgery

Most patients think that deciding to have bariatric surgery is one of the hardest things they have ever had to do. Many people in their lives allegedly give them advice on choices, whether or not they directly want it, according to the vast majority of patients. Patients report this regardless of whether they specifically requested this information or not. You should have faith in your ability to get over self-doubt even if others have tried to motivate you but were unsuccessful. Have faith in your abilities and chances for success. You weren't given the option to make it or intentionally choose it; rather, you were forced to make the choice, which will have an impact on your life and health.

This choice was approved by a group of highly qualified medical experts who offer patients guidance based on knowledge and conclusions drawn from the most recent studies. That is, the advantages of following a particular course of action outweigh the disadvantages of doing nothing at all, as shown by historical precedent and empirical facts that support the medical advice. If you continue to go forward at your current pace, the benefits will so soon begin to manifest one at a time and occasionally in huge groups all at once. Therefore, never question a decision you've already made, regardless of how it may feel to you right now.

Why should people have pleasure in the food they eat?

It's hard to conceive that you'll ever look forward to a meal again when you wake up from surgery and realize that the majority of what you're consuming is fluids. When you are still healing from the anesthetic and other after-effects of the procedure, this is particularly true in the first few days after surgery. On the surface, eating could seem like a chore that must be completed because it's necessary for survival. However, if you are constantly telling yourself, "I need to get my protein in, I need to drink more water," it is easy to lose interest in the flavors and joys of the food you eat. Undoubtedly, you are wondering when and when you'll feel like eating again. Will I ever be able to enjoy the foods I always cherished and frequently anticipated?

Remember that just after surgery, your body will experience a flurry of physiological and hormonal changes that will affect how much food you can consume and how hungry you feel. These alterations will cause a decline in both your capacity to consume food and your appetite. The majority of the early, significant weight loss you notice after making these changes can probably be attributed to lifestyle changes. Please do your best to be patient. Over time, your body will change, allowing you to have a stronger appetite and the ability to eat a wider variety of meals. All of these beneficial changes will occur if you consume a diet that is reduced in fat and higher in fruits and vegetables.

The good news is that in a few months, you will have established a foundation of eating habits and exercise regimens that will help you lose weight permanently. The good news is that it appears you can keep off the weight you've steadily lost. news that is good, indeed! Some patients claim that after surgery, the acute cravings for foods like burgers and fries they had before the treatment have completely vanished. Patients who craved these foods voraciously before surgery experience this. Some claim that their appetites for certain foods have completely vanished after surgery. Despite the fact that numerous patients have asserted this to be the truth, I can see why you might dismiss this as absurd. Your body will start to crave more nutrient-dense meals as you transition from a diet strong in fat, sugar, and salt to one rich in wholesome foods. Your body is transitioning from a diet that is low in nutritious foods to one that is high in nutritious meals, which is why this is happening. This occurs as your body starts to recognize the benefits of certain foods. And now is the perfect moment to experiment with adapting some of your all-time favorite recipes to fit a healthier lifestyle. If you enjoy cooking, now is a great time to experiment with different spices and flavors to ensure diversity in your protein choices and to introduce this new way of living to your family. This is also a great chance to expose your children to this new way of life if you have any. If you have kids, now is the greatest time to introduce them to this new way of life. However, this new way of living might be advantageous to those without families.

Whether or not you have ever spent a lot of time in the kitchen, there are a number of easy and economical alternatives that will allow you to eat healthily without putting in a lot of effort on your behalf. This is true even if you don't have much culinary experience. Making sure that a regular number of calories are ingested each day is crucial because food is the body's main source of energy. On the other hand, eating involves much more than merely providing our bodies with nourishment. Moments of connection can be shared by doing things like eating dinner as a family, celebrating an anniversary with a candlelight dinner, making new friends at a church picnic, and remembering the meals Grandma used to make. The setting you choose is just as important as the food itself in ensuring that you enjoy yourself while dining. If you're prepared to put in a little effort, persist, and have an open mind to exploring new foods after surgery, you and your family can start eating healthy meals.

One Cookbook with Every Type of Surgical and Non-Surgical Weight Loss Method

This recipe book is being kindly given to you. The nutritional requirements of patients who have undergone surgeries like the Roux-en-Y gastric bypass, sleeve gastrectomy, laparoscopic adjustable gastric band implantation, or biliopancreatic diversion with duodenal switch (BPD/DS) have been carefully considered when creating each meal. The following patients underwent these procedures: The dietary guidance was created as a reference from recommendations made by the American Society of Metabolic and Bariatric Surgery and the Academy of Nutrition and Dietetics based on relevant research. They shouldn't be used as a substitute for the advice provided by your medical team. On the basis of the findings of the field research, you have been given diet recommendations. Every medical treatment is unique, just as every person experiences post-operative eating differently. There is therefore no diet that is appropriate for individuals of all ages and lifestyles.

To meet your weight-loss and nutritional goals—while continuing to enjoy great dishes without compromising flavor—use this guide as a comprehensive review of how to handle eating, food choices, portion sizes, and cooking after surgery. By using the ideas in this book, you can reach your objectives without sacrificing flavor. Using the information in this book, you can accomplish your goals without sacrificing enjoyment. The majority of the dietary suggestions for the process that follows are essentially the same, with a few minor variations that will be discussed throughout this chapter. This chapter will go into great detail about these variations. These kinds of circumstances are not common. Any further advice given should be carefully considered and followed after every meal. These suggestions will provide more thorough guidance on the ideal times to introduce each specialty food into your lifestyle. While you meet with your medical team, you should bring this book along so you may use it as a resource when making meal plans and preparing ready for adjustments to the consistency of the foods you eat. You will receive assistance from your medical team while you adjust to the new meals you will be eating.

Years of Practice Developed Bariatric Nutrition Expertise

Most patients will have at least tried one of the several weight-loss programs available before having bariatric surgery. Most people find it so uncomfortable that they fear having to learn all the specifics of yet another meal plan. As a result, your newfound understanding of how to eat after bariatric surgery will be built on the knowledge you have gathered from prior attempts at dieting. Consequently, a thorough understanding of nutrition is not required to comprehend and effectively apply a bariatric eating plan.

Let's examine how this cookbook's various recipes correspond to the post-surgery nutrition guidelines. To begin with, you should eat more of these meals if you want to lose weight.

Liquids.

The first and most important piece of advice that should be followed after surgery is to drink lots of water. Your overall level of energy will rise if you drink enough fluids, but you'll also see that this exercise really supports your efforts to reduce your body fat percentage. Your general level of energy will rise if you drink enough water. The most frequent post-operative issue is dehydration, but it may be prevented with a few simple safety precautions and preventative measures. Since you can't drink during meals or for at least 30 minutes before or after each meal when you first start, it could be challenging. Every meal must be had at least an hour before you can drink anything. Never underestimate the significance of taking precautions and always having a drink with you.

To prevent the uncomfortable scenario of having to make up for lost time later, it is essential to maintain a steady fluid intake throughout the day and into the evening. You won't be able to fast devour a sizable amount of food or drink all at once, as you typically would, because you have a handy bag.

The following list of beverages can be consumed: Water, milk, soy milk, protein shakes, decaffeinated coffee or tea (without cream or sugar), as well as any other noncarbonated, sugar-free liquids, are acceptable beverages (sweetened with sugar substitutes are okay)

The suggested daily intake range for your post-operative diet should be between 64 and 100 ounces when you first start, and it should gradually rise as you go.

Fruit juices, caffeinated drinks (including soda, coffee, tea, and energy drinks), carbonated waters, alcoholic drinks, lemonade, sweetened tea, sugary sports drinks, and other liquids containing sugar should be used sparingly or avoided.

Protein.

Protein should be consumed immediately after surgery because it is the macronutrient that can be gotten with the least amount of effort. The majority of muscle and tissue is made up of protein, which also serves a structural purpose.

Maintaining a diet high in protein and low in calories is crucial. If you eat enough protein, you will feel fuller for longer after meals, have more energy, and burn more fat while preserving your muscle mass. Dairy products, meat, fish, eggs, and poultry are all sources of protein. Protein digests more slowly even though it contains more calories than fat. Unlike carbohydrates, protein is also absorbed more gradually. On how to recuperate from surgery, including how much water to drink and how to concentrate on eating meals that are high in protein for the first few days, precise instructions will be given to you. You will unavoidably start eating more meals that include a wider variety of foods as your degree of physical fitness increases.

This cookbook is essential because it provides you with a variety of recipes that will enable you to eat the right quantity of protein over a long period of time without growing tired of your food. The cookbook contains these concepts. Protein should be consumed at every meal for the remainder of one's life in order to maintain one's current weight over time without gaining weight. Protein should also be consumed if you want to slim down and get in shape.

Eggs, poultry, all forms of fish and seafood, low-fat dairy items, such as low-fat Greek yogurt, 1% or nonfat cottage cheese, 1% or nonfat milk and cheese, and lean beef (if tolerated, starting three months after surgery; sirloin, loin, round roast or steak, and lean or supremely lean ground beef) are all advised (beans, nuts, lentils, and seeds)

The daily dietary allowance is between 60 and 100 grams. (It's important to remember that particular recommendations vary on the patient's target weight and the stage of the post-operative diet.)

Among the foods that should either be consumed in moderation or avoided are high-fat dairy products like cream and whole milk, high-fat beef or pig cuts (such as pork sausage and bacon, bologna, salami, pork ribs, and ground beef), skin-on poultry breasts, and chicken breasts.

You'll be required to drink a protein smoothie every day for a few days or weeks following surgery. This will carry on all the way through recovery. Finding enough sources of protein may be a full-time job for some people. If you don't have access to any liquid sources of protein, it could be challenging for you to meet your daily needs. Since it is doubtful that you would consume protein shakes for breakfast, lunch, and dinner every day for the rest of your life, we want to develop a long-term healthy eating plan instead. Because of this, our focus should be on creating a nutritious diet. We must therefore ensure that we have a plan in place for cooking wholesome meals. To make it simpler for the patient to eat full meals, I would advise beginning the pureed diet as soon as it is safe to do so after surgery. If you're searching for something to do in between meals, milk may be a better choice than protein beverages from the supermarket. It will be difficult to eat a lot during the first few weeks after surgery, so you should concentrate most of your efforts on meals high in high-quality protein sources. You should be aware that liquid food digests more slowly than solid food and needs fewer calories. So think carefully about it before attempting to prepare pureed turkey chili. Those who have undergone bariatric surgery may use the following protein powders:

Whey protein isolate is a great source of protein for your diet. The protein in this form has all nine essential amino acids and is the easiest to enter your body.

These sources, all of the very best quality, are given below: Egg white powder and vegan soy protein isolate are the only two ingredients in this product.

Test the product in its most basic form. Since they have fewer calories than other foods and don't contain any potentially dangerous additives that are typically found in other meals, these are healthier selections.

The following suggestions could be utilized to create various flavor variations: Choose items that are completely sugar-free and sweetened with stevia, sucralose (Splenda), or other sweeteners rather than using regular table sugar. There are hundreds of options, from vanilla to butter pecan, and each one will satisfy you even if you only consume a little number of calories overall. The ice cream contains these flavors. They have no calories, can be consumed often after surgery, and have never been linked in studies to the onset of dumping syndrome. They are a fantastic option because the FDA has approved their use. Sugar alcohols like erythritol, mannitol, xylitol, and sorbitol should be used with extreme caution because they contain calories and may produce unpleasant gastrointestinal side effects in some people.

Carbohydrates.

Carbohydrates, a rapid source of energy, are mostly used by your body's metabolic processes, especially those in your brain. This is accurate since glucose, the body's main fuel source, can only be produced when carbohydrates are present. You will therefore be instructed to have little or no carbohydrate in the days immediately following surgery.

Your body will keep working as it should if it gets its energy from the breakdown of internal fat stores and consumes the protein you eat at meals. There are two types of carbohydrates: basic and complicated. Simple carbohydrates can be easily divided into smaller components. We experience an energy surge from simple carbohydrates, which is followed by a crash. Due to how quickly and easily they are absorbed and converted to sugar in the blood, this occurs. Simple carbohydrates are said to be present in a number of processed foods, candies, sodas, juice drinks, and meals made with white refined flour. The body processes complex carbohydrates more slowly than simple ones because they contain more fiber, vitamins, and minerals. This justification for selecting complex carbs. Along with fruits and vegetables, this category also includes meals made with nutritious grains. You should therefore consume more complex carbohydrates overall while ingesting less simple carbohydrates overall.

Examples of typical foods that can be consumed are as follows: Other suitable foods include raw fruit, potatoes with skin (sweet or white), brown or wild rice, 100% whole-wheat pasta (if tolerated), barley, and ancient grains (if tolerated). Rather of doughy raw potatoes, toasted whole-grain foods are preferable (quinoa, spelled, farrow, and millet)

In terms of daily portions, start out slowly; over time, try to have no more than 35 to 45 percent of your total calories come from carbohydrates.

Foods made of white refined grains, including chips, sweets, cakes, pastries, biscuits, beverages (including fruit juice), and sodas, should all be consumed in moderation, if not entirely avoided.

regarding sugar.

The body's capacity to digest simple carbohydrates is decreased after surgery. After consuming meals that are heavy in sugar or, in extremely rare circumstances, after inhaling a very big amount of carbs all at once, dumping syndrome is a condition that can occur. These two possibilities are incredibly unlikely to come true. After consuming the contaminated food, symptoms such as shaking, lightheadedness, sweating, or dizziness (with a risk of fainting), an elevated heart rate, a drop in blood sugar (reactive hypoglycemia), stomach cramps, and diarrhea may emerge immediately. An individual is more likely to experience dumping syndrome than the average person if they have had Roux-en-Y gastric bypass surgery, borderline personality disorder, or an eating disorder. A sleeve gastrectomy patient may likewise experience this negative outcome. To avoid this excruciating illness, stay away from meals that are high in sugar. It can be avoided by eating foods high in sugar. If at all possible, try to avoid processed foods that contain more than 10 to 15 grams of sugar per serving. This can be used as a broad rule of thumb. Remember that fruits and dairy products both contain trace levels of naturally occurring sugars if you want to lead a healthy lifestyle.

Fats.

Without the lipids included in meals, the body is unable to absorb the fat-soluble vitamins A, D, E, and K. The body needs each of these fat-soluble vitamins for healthy health. For instance, human bodies are unable to produce omega-3s and omega-6s on their own; as a result, these fatty acids must be consumed through diet. Even when we eat meals that are seen as better substitutes to fried foods, we should continuously be aware of how much food we consume because fats have the highest calorie density of any macronutrient (9 calories are contained in 1 gram of fat). Avoid eating prepared foods with low-fat or fat-free labels since, typically, the flavor that the fat provides is substituted by the addition of more sugar or salt to enhance the dish's overall appeal. Low-fat or fat-free dairy products like milk, yogurt, and cottage cheese may help with the consumption of less calories and less saturated fat, which can prevent heart attacks and strokes by avoiding plaque accumulation in the arteries. When it is possible to do so when cooking, you should employ these various adjustments of the recipes. Nonfat and milk with a percent less fat both contain the same amount of protein per gram as whole milk, and neither has less important nutrients. Fatty fish, avocados, nuts, seeds, vegetable oils, nuts and seeds, olives, avocados, and even olive oil are heart-healthy items to include in your diet.

How to Recharge Avocados, canola oil, chia seeds, fatty fish (such as salmon, mackerel, and tuna), shellfish, flaxseed, olive oil, almonds, walnuts, peanuts, and natural nut butters are just a few of the many healthy foods that are widely available. Flaxseed, olives, and natural nut butter are more examples of foods that are nutrient-dense. The other three meal options are shellfish, flaxseed, and olives.

How much food is eaten each day: Starting out with extremely small amounts, fewer than 30% of your daily calories should come from fat (primarily from monounsaturated and polyunsaturated fats, and less than 7% from saturated fats). Avoid eating food that has the following ingredients: Butter, oils derived from tropical fruits (including palm and coconut oil), full-fat dairy products, and a variety of vegetable oils are examples of healthy fats.

Reduce your intake of fried foods, trans-fat-containing margarine, lard, other animal fats, and meals that are high in saturated and trans fats. Additionally, meals rich in animal fats like lard and pig fat are to be avoided.

There is no doubting the existence of dietary supplements like vitamins and minerals.

Due to modifications in the amount of food they may eat and the manner some nutrients are absorbed, all bariatric surgery patients must take vitamin and mineral supplements after their procedure. Even though food will still be your body's primary supply of nutrients after having bariatric surgery, it won't be the best source of nutrients any longer. You can get vitamin and mineral recommendations from your primary care doctor. One of the recommendations made by the team who conducted your bariatric surgery is that you should take great care to adhere to the specified limitations.

Those who are having surgery ought to take a multivitamin with minerals. The tablet may be a chewable or liquid. Verify the vitamin and mineral content to make sure it contains between 100 and 200 percent of each nutrient's daily recommended intake. This will ensure that you are receiving the proper dosage of each.

The majority of patients are encouraged to take vitamin D supplements prior to surgery since nearly all patients who are eligible for the therapy have insufficient vitamin D levels.

Post-operative patients almost often receive the recommendation to take calcium supplements since calcium is essential for maintaining bone health.

Iron supplements are routinely prescribed to patients who have recently undergone gastric bypass surgery, such as the Roux-en-Y operation or BPD/DS, as part of a typical treatment plan. This is due to the physiological changes caused by these operations, which impair the body's capacity to absorb iron.

Particularly after a Roux-en-Y gastric bypass, BPD/DS treatment, or potentially even a sleeve gastrectomy, vitamin B1/2 supplements are advised. After a sleeve gastrectomy, it could also be advised to take vitamin B1/2 supplements. It is necessary for healthy nerve function and to prevent anemia, which could arise in the absence of it. Without it, a condition like anemia could arise.

You should begin taking a nutritional supplement with specialized fat-soluble vitamins as soon as you finish the BPD/DS. With your team, you must discuss this idea.

After undergoing any kind of bariatric surgery, including gastric bypass, patients may be advised to take B-complex vitamins as a supplement supply of B vitamins. Thiamine, a mineral required for the efficient functioning of the metabolism, may be present in this material in high proportions.

Due to the nature of these therapies, it is essential to continue taking specialized vitamin and mineral supplements for the rest of one's life. When patients reached their ideal weight but stopped taking their vitamins at the same time, impairments started to show up years later. This idea has crossed my mind a couple of times in the past.

You must continue to set up routine follow-up appointments with your healthcare providers so they can monitor the concentrations of these essential nutrients in your blood.

Equipment.

The vast majority of the recipes in this book can be made using only a cutting board and a sauté pan, with the exception of a good knife. The most essential kitchen equipment that you must own in order to effectively prepare some of the recipes in this cookbook is listed in the list below. These ingredients are necessary for you to complete some of the recipes. The most of them, as well as the others, are easily offered by sizable department stores, where they are also reasonably priced.

Any cuisine you prepare, be it soup, chili, or something completely different, may be transformed into a velvety puree using the proper technique. All that is needed is a hand blender or an immersion blender.

A mini-blender or food processor is acceptable for use in the microwave but not the dishwasher. To bring food with you while you're out and about, purée little servings or blend one into a smoothie.

a little muffin pan These baked goods are excellent for regulating portion amounts because they are manageable due to their smaller size.

Crockpots and conventional slow cookers are both referred to as "slow cookers" in this section. However, it has been decided that the recipes in this book call for a pot with a capacity of 5 quarts. Of course, you are free to change the quantity of food you prepare in line with your own preferences.

Using a kitchen tool called a spiralizer, zucchini may be made into noodles instead of regular spaghetti. Spiralizers that are portable are quite useful.

Fruits and vegetables that must be avoided for the first few months after surgery can have their rough skins removed using a vegetable peeler. Any fruits or vegetables with rough skins should be avoided at this time. With the use of this tool, the tough fruit and vegetable skins can be removed with ease.

Advice for reaching your goals and prospering in life

The following postoperative instructions have been given to you in the hopes that they would assist you in ensuring that you not only reach your goal weight but also maintain it over time. The following advice has a history of helping people reach their weight loss objectives, in accordance with my years of experience working with happy post-bariatric surgery patients who have maintained a healthy lifestyle for more than five years.

You should decide to keep visiting your bariatric clinic as soon as possible and stick with it.

The specialists in this field know what to look for to ensure that you can maintain your healthy lifestyle and ward off issues over time. A community general practitioner may choose to ignore a routine therapy that a bariatric clinic deems unnecessary or insignificant.

Just stroll outside for some exercise and fresh air.

If the patient has rapid weight loss after surgery, they can be tempted to stop engaging in physically demanding activities. Walking is the exercise that post-operative patients participate in repeatedly over the long term, despite the fact that it may appear very simple. So buckle up, prepare for the adventure, and tighten your shoes.

Make sure you are getting enough protein in your diet.

It could be tempting to return to a pattern where breakfast is cereal and lunch is a sandwich with some filling in between the slices of bread after recovering from surgery for a few years. However, this might not be the best option for your long-term health. On the other hand, you shouldn't if you frequently eat again. You start to notice that you are progressively regaining the weight after around 30 minutes. This might occur extremely quickly. Make sure you obtain enough protein in at least half of each meal as your long-term objective. Every meal should contain a range of meals for the other half in order to keep things interesting and preserve a healthy balance.

Each drop of liquid has a specific weight.

Drinking a lot of water before and after meals is a smart move if you don't want to feel hungry in between meals. You might be able to stop undesirable habits like mindless snacking and overeating during meals by doing this. Make it a long-term goal to get a water bottle you like using and drink 100 ounces or more of water every day. Fluid loading may be a highly efficient strategy to assist minimize the amount of food consumed at one meal after the first six months have elapsed following surgery. This can be done to help limit the amount of food consumed. Even though you shouldn't drink anything during or after your meal, you should have a glass of water within 10 minutes of sitting down to eat. You won't feel as though your stomach is full if you do this. If you take this advice, you'll probably eat fewer calories overall and have greater satisfaction. Keep in mind that you shouldn't begin drinking until six months after your surgery, and then only 10 minutes before a meal. This allows your body to properly metabolize alcohol, which takes longer to digest than food.

Find a support network for those who have undergone bariatric surgery.

Joining a support group can help you build a network of friends who will be there for you throughout your life. After you attain your ideal weight, your adventure won't be over; instead, you should join a support group. Even when you have reached your ideal weight, work still needs to be done. You might want to lead by example for others or you might need someone to listen to you with empathy. These two possibilities are both conceivable.

You Need to Continue Eating Well for the Rest of Your Life.

You already have everything you need to set up an effective weight-loss plan for yourself, so there's no need to buy anything new. Your relationship with food has probably been the furthest thing from your thoughts throughout your life, and there's a good probability that it brings you a lot of headaches and other unpleasant feelings. On the other side, you might restore that connection and rewire your brain to stop you from swiftly slipping back into your old habits. You should start by giving yourself little, manageable goals that you can achieve once a week, and work your way up from there. The best strategy for success is this. Congratulate yourself when you make progress, but don't berate yourself if you can't finish a task in a given amount of time. Instead, concentrate on creating new, more realistic objectives. Continuously challenging yourself will keep you inspired to try new things. You must commit to leading a healthy lifestyle for the rest of your life after having bariatric surgery. If you consciously work to keep your promises to eat better and exercise more, you may maintain your improved way of life for a sizable amount of time.

Chapter Two

Dietary

Protein Shake with Iced Coffee.

Do you find it difficult to give up your favorite cup of java first thing in the morning? Having a cup of black decaffeinated coffee after surgery is something that most dietitians would recommend, and this is accurate (no added cream or sugars, of course). Although it is suggested that patients refrain from consuming caffeine and avoid sugary, high-calorie coffee beverages until they have a firm grasp on the post-operative diet and are drinking adequate water, this is not always possible. The good news is that you can still get your caffeine fix by drinking this protein shake with coffee flavoring.

- One scoop (1/4 cup) vanilla protein powder (optional)

- 1 cup decaffeinated coffee, freshly made and served cold 1 cup skim milk (or nonfat milk)

- 1/2 teaspoon ground cinnamon

- 1/2 cup ice cubes

- Pour the milk into a blender and mix until smooth. Add the protein powder, cinnamon, and ice and blend until smooth. Blend on high speed for 3 to 4 minutes or until the smoothie is smooth and the protein powder has been completely dissolved, depending on your blender.

- Refrigerate any shakes that aren't consumed or used straight away, and reblend them just before serving. After seven days, throw away any leftover shakes.

Serving Size (in ounces): Calories in a serving: 102 0 g of total fat Sodium: 155 milligrams Carbohydrates in total: 8 g 6 g of sugar 0g of dietary fiber 1/4 g of protein

Chocolate Protein Shake for Chocolate Lovers.

Chocolate is one of the most popular sweet treats of all time. Even a modest amount of food can stimulate the production of feel-good endorphins in our brain, such as serotonin. Fortunately, there is a method to satisfy your chocolate cravings without consuming the excessive amounts of sugar present in most chocolate-based products. Make this shake, which has a chocolate taste from protein powder and the cocoa powder, and you'll be in a chocolate lover's paradise in minutes.

- 1 cup skim milk (or nonfat milk)

- 1/2 cup low-fat cottage cheese (optional)

- protein powder, either chocolate or plain, one scoop (1/4 cup) 2 tablespoons cocoa powder (unsweetened is best)

- 1/2 teaspoons of pure vanilla essence and five cubes of ice

- Put all the ingredients in a blender and mix on high for 2 to 3 minutes until the drink is smooth and all the powders are completely dissolved. Pour the shake into a glass and serve immediately.

- Pour half of the shake into a glass and serve immediately.

- Refrigerate any shakes that aren't consumed or used straight away, and reblend them just before serving. After seven days, throw away any leftover shakes.

- Cacao beans, from which chocolate is derived, are rich in antioxidants and protective flavonols, which benefit the heart and circulatory system. Unfortunately, most chocolate used in desserts is filled with added fats and sugar and contains little of the actual cocoa bean. It is possible to make low-carb cakes and candies out of 100 percent unsweetened cocoa powder; however, you should consider combining it with milk to obtain the antioxidants and chocolate fix without the sugar.

Serving Size (in ounces): Calories in this recipe: 188 5 g of total fat Sodium: 38 milligrams Carbohydrates in total: 1/4g 3 g of sugar 2 g of dietary fiber 25 g of protein

Mint Dream Protein Shake

Let's travel back to the 1950s, when ice cream beverages were all the rage. Dinner wasn't complete unless it was followed up with a cold, creamy dessert like a Grasshopper, a blend of sweet chocolate, vanilla ice cream, and mint liqueur, among other ingredients. Try this Mint Dream Shake (which, yes, is alcohol-free) as a perfectly lovely alternative for your favorite cocktail. Include the hidden ingredient, a handful of fresh spinach, to give this drink an extra dose of nutrition while remaining completely undetectable. This smoothie may be consumed after supper to fulfill your sweet taste while meeting your daily protein requirements.

- One little handful (about) (less than 1 cup) of spinach that has been freshly harvested

- 1 cup skim milk (or nonfat milk)

- One scoop (1/4 cup) vanilla protein powder (optional)

- 1/4 cup plain Greek yogurt with no added sugar

- One tablespoon of cocoa powder (optional)

- 1/2tsp peppermint essential oil

- Three cubes of ice

- 2 to 3 sprigs of fresh mint for garnishing

- To make the smoothie, place all the ingredients in a blender and process on high for 3 to 4 minutes or until the spinach is completely pureed and all the powders are dissolved (about 3 to 4 minutes).

- Pour half of the shake into a glass, garnish with the fresh mint sprigs, and serve immediately to enjoy.

- Refrigerate any shakes that aren't consumed or used straight away, and reblend them just before serving. After one day, throw away any remaining shakes.

- Spinach is a great source of iron, as is broccoli. Iron absorption in the body is hindered after a Roux-en-Y gastric bypass (also known as BPD), and many patients require iron supplements after having this procedure. Add a handful of spinach to your next protein smoothie to help you meet your iron requirements. Meats and beans are excellent suppliers of iron, as are other legumes.

Calories per cup (1 cup serving): 135 calories 1 gram of total fat Sodium: 115 milligrams Carbohydrates in total: 1/2g 8 g of sugar 1 gram of fiber 18 g of protein

Protein Shake in the flavor of Dreamsicle.

Nothing says "refreshing" quite like the taste of fresh citrus fruits. Chocolate and vanilla might get monotonous after a while, so give your taste buds pleasure by indulging in something with a sweet orange aroma and flavor. Using this protein shake, you can have the creamy orange flavor of an Orange Julius without having to eat it. Cottage cheese is an important component, not only because it provides protein but also because it contributes to the ultra-creamy texture of the dish.

- 1/2 cups ice cubes

- 1/2 cup low-fat cottage cheese (optional)

- 2 to 4 teaspoons extra water if necessary, plus 1/2 cup water

- 1 tangerine or mandarin orange (about 2 ounces) or 1 small mandarin orange fruit cup (approximately 1 cup), drained

- 1 scoop (about 1/4 cup) Protein powder that is unflavored or vanilla in taste 1 teaspoon stevia extract (in powdered form)

- 1/2 teaspoon of pure vanilla essence

- Blend the ice, cottage cheese, water, tangerine, protein powder, stevia, and vanilla on high speed for 2 to 3 minutes or until the smoothie is smooth and no longer has lumps in it. If the shake is too thick, add 2 to 4 teaspoons of water.

- Pour half of the shake into a glass and serve immediately.

- Refrigerate any shakes that aren't consumed or used straight away, and reblendthem just before serving. After seven days, throw away any leftover shakes.

Per serving (1 cup), there are the following calories: Calories consumed: 137 1 gram of total fat Sodium: 104 milligrams Carbohydrates in total: 1/2 g 8 g of sugar 1 gram of fiber 21 g of protein

Protein Shake with Strawberry Crème.

Do you have a strawberry milkshake on your mind? By switching to this version, you may avoid eating the equivalent of a day's worth of calories in a single drink. The Greek yogurt gives this shake a creamy texture similar to that of an ice cream shake from your neighborhood ice cream shop. Using frozen strawberries will result in a thicker, more melted combination, while fresh strawberries would result in a thinner, more melted mixture.

- 1 cup low-fat milk or unsweetened soy milk (or a combination thereof) 1 cup strawberries, either fresh or frozen

- 1/2 cup plain Greek yogurt with no added sugar

- 1 scoop (1/4 cup) protein powder, either vanilla or unflavored

- 1/2 teaspoon of pure vanilla essence

- Blend the milk, strawberries, yogurt, protein powder, and vanilla in a blender for 2 to 3 minutes or until the drink is smooth and the protein powder has been completely dissolved.

- Pour half of the shake into a glass and serve immediately.

- Refrigerate any shakes that aren't consumed or used straight away, and reblend them just before serving. After seven days, throw away any leftover shakes.

Per serving (1 cup), there are the following calories: Calories in a serving: 1/45 2 g of total fat Sodium: 92 milligrams Carbohydrates in total: 15 g 6 g of sugar 1 gram of fiber 15 g of protein

Protein Shake with Cherries and Almonds.

This delectable shake features characteristics that are similar to the original cherries jubilee and will satisfy your demands for a creamy cherry fix in a great way. Not only does it save you money, especially during the off-season, but it also lends this shake a creamier texture because of the use of frozen fruit. Is there no almond extract available in the house? If you're in a hurry, vanilla extract can be substituted.

- 1 cup (5.3 ounces) low-fat black cherry yogurt (optional) (see tip)
- 1/2 cup of water
- 1/2 cup skim milk or nonfat milk
- 1/4 cup frozen pitted cherries (drained)
- 1 scoop (about 1/4 cup) of Protein powder in either vanilla or plain flavor
- 1/2 teaspoon almond extract (optional)

- Blend on high speed for 2 to 3 minutes to incorporate the yogurt, water, milk, cherries, protein powder, and almond extract in a blender until the smoothie is smooth and the protein powder is completely dissolved.

- Pour half of the shake into a glass and serve immediately.

- Refrigerate any shakes that aren't consumed or used straight away, and reblend them just before serving. After seven days, throw away any leftover shakes.

- Make your flavorings out of ordinary ingredients wherever feasible. For example, use stevia extract, sugar-free fruit preserves, sugar-free pudding mix, cocoa powder, or cinnamon to add taste without adding additional sugars to your baked goods. Following a typical post-operative diet, you can sweeten plain yogurt with fresh fruit. If you're looking for flavored Greek yogurt selections with the least amount of sugar possible while providing adequate protein, read the labels carefully. Fewer than 10 grams of sugar and more than 1/2 grams of protein per serving are preferable.

Per serving (1 cup), there are the following calories: Calories in a serving: 158 1 gram of total fat Sodium: 89 milligrams Carbohydrates in total: 16 g 1/2 g of sugar 0g of dietary fiber 20 g of protein

Smoothie with chocolate and peanut butter.

A Reese's Peanut Butter Cup, or possibly a chocolate–peanut butter ice cream sundae, would be just what the doctor ordered. So go no further than this recipe for a low-calorie, low-carb solution that will fulfill your craving for peanut butter bliss. Chocolate and creamy peanut butter come together in this protein smoothie to create a drink that is both delicious and nutritious. Finally, your craving has been quenched!

- 1 cup skim milk (or nonfat milk)

- 1/2 cup plain Greek yogurt with no added sugar

- 1 scoop (1/4 cup) vanilla protein powder (optional), Peanut butter powder (about 2 teaspoons), cocoa powder (about 2 teaspoons)

- To make the chocolate protein shake, place the ingredients in a blender and process on high for 3 to 4 minutes until the protein powder, powdered peanut butter, and cocoa powder are completely dissolved.

- Half of the smoothie should be poured into a glass and enjoyed.

- Refrigerate any smoothies that aren't going to be consumed or used right away, thenreblend them just before serving. After seven days, throw away any leftover smoothie.

- Even while this smoothie is good for a complete liquid diet during the first few days and weeks after surgery, it also serves as a fantastic source of additional protein over the long run. Drink it after dinner to help you reach your protein objectives or as a delectable dessert replacement.

Serving Size (in ounces): Calories in this recipe: 185 3 g of total fat Sodium: 173 milligrams

Carbohydrates in total: 17g 10 g of sugar 3 g of dietary fiber 24 g of protein

Smoothie with Pumpkin Flavoring.

When the leaves change color and the temperature begins to chill, you crave pumpkin everything—pumpkin spiced lattes, pumpkin pies, and even pumpkin cheesecake. But where do you begin? When you have this creamy smoothie, which is rich in protein and pumpkin flavor and low in sugar, you don't need to worry about losing out on these delectable goodies. Because cottage cheese is unnoticeable, it contributes to this smoothie's smooth, creamy texture. Pumpkin is a powerhouse of nutrients, including the antioxidants vitamin A and beta-carotene, as well as a significant amount of fiber. In addition to using pumpkin puree to make sweet meals, you can thicken savory foods, such as your favorite chili recipe, to give a touch of sweetness and thicken the consistency.

- 1 cup low-fat milk or unsweetened soy milk (or a combination thereof)

- 1/2 cup pumpkin puree (optional)

- 1/2 cup low-fat cottage cheese (optional)

- 1 scoop (1/4 cup) protein powder (unflavored or vanilla flavor) Pumpkin pie spice (around 1 teaspoon)

- 1 teaspoon pure vanilla extract (optional)

- Blend the milk, pumpkin puree, cottage cheese, protein powder, pumpkin pie spice, and vanilla in a blender on high speed for 2 to 3 minutes, or until the smoothie is smooth and the protein powder is completely dissolved until the powder is completely dissolved.

- Half of the smoothie should be poured into a glass and enjoyed.

- Refrigerate any smoothies that aren't going to be consumed or used right away, thenreblend them just before serving. After seven days, throw away any leftover smoothie.

- The canned pumpkin puree may be found in the baking aisle at your local supermarket. If you like, you may bake a little pie pumpkin and use it instead of buying one. Cut the pumpkin in half, remove and discard the stem, pulp, and seeds, and arrange the pieces cut-side down on a baking sheet covered with cooking spray. Bake for 30 minutes. Baking at 350°F for about 60 minutes, or until the flesh is cooked and can be mashed or pureed, will yield a tender and flavorful result.

Per serving (1 cup), there are the following calories: Calories: 196 calories: 2 g of total fat Sodium: 392 milligrams Carbohydrates in total: 17g 6 g of sugar 3 g of dietary fiber 25 g of protein

Ricotta Cheese with a Sweet Cinnamon-Vanilla Flavour.

Italian cuisine is synonymous with comfort; nothing screams comfort food like a delicious Italian dessert. Of course, eating Italian pastries is out of the question on a diet. Still, this creamy ricotta cheese can trick your tastebuds into believing you've just had silky, delectable cannoli filling. If you want to give it a chocolate flavoring, you can sprinkle on some 100 percent cocoa powder.

- 1 cup ricotta cheese (preferably low-fat) 1 teaspoon pure vanilla extract (optional)

- 1 teaspoon of cinnamon, ground 1 teaspoon of freshly grated nutmeg

- 1/2 teaspoon stevia extract (in powdered form)

- To make the ricotta cheese, place it in a small container with an airtight cover and stir for 1 minute or until the spices are evenly dispersed throughout it (about 1 minute total).

- Serve immediately, or chill overnight for an even more taste the next day.

- In addition to being high in protein, both ricotta and cottage cheese are also low in calories, especially the low-fat varieties. Aside from that, they are exceedingly well tolerated throughout the first several days and weeks following surgery. Mix low-sugar spaghetti sauce with ricotta cheese to make a delicious ricotta delicacy that can be served as a lasagna without needing noodles. Try mixing in some Taco Seasoning and cottage cheese for a Southwest-inspired variation, or toss in some dried onions and chives for a finishing touch.

Calories per serving (1/2 cup): 116 Calories per serving 5 g of total fat Sodium: 1/40 milligrams Carbohydrates in total: 6g 4 g of sugar 0g of dietary fiber 13 g of protein

Pinto Beans with Cheddar Cheese

While large burritos are out of the question, this dish captures the beany, cheesy essence of what makes them so addicting in their simplicity and simplicity. Vegetarian refried beans are a fantastic source of protein and fiber, two nutrients required in large quantities after surgery. Beans are a very affordable source of protein; have cans of beans on hand for the first few days following surgery, or simply whip up a quick lunch whenever the mood strikes you.

- Drain and rinse 1 pinto bean can (15 ounces), and set aside. 1 tablespoon lime juice that has been freshly squeezed

- 1 teaspoon Taco Seasoning (optional)

- Cheddar, Mexican mix, or pepper jack cheese (about 1/4 cup) Jack

- Heat the beans in a small saucepan over medium-low heat, occasionally stirring, until they are heated throughout, about 5 minutes. Turn the heat down to a bare minimum. Mix in the lime juice and taco spice until everything is well-combined.

- To get the required consistency, purée the beans in a blender or immersion blender until smooth, or mash them with a potato masher until smooth.

- Before serving, sprinkle the cheese on top of the beans and toss to combine.

- These delicious refried beans are ideal for the puree period following surgery. Powdered egg whites or unflavored protein powder can be mixed to enhance the amount of protein in the dish.

Per serving (1/4 cup): calories: 230 Calories in a serving: 1/23 3 g of total fat 421 milligrams of sodium Carbohydrates in total: 18g 0 g of sugar 5 g of dietary fiber 7 g of protein

Scrambled eggs

Step-by-step instructions on creating the ideal scrambled eggs are included, along with suggestions for luring them up.

- Cooking spray with a nonstick coating

- 2 quail eggs

- low-fat milk (about 1 tablespoon)

- 1/2 teaspoon thyme leaves (dry) peppercorns that have been freshly ground

- Preheat a small pan over medium heat, spraying the bottom of the skillet with cooking spray before adding the ingredients.

- Lightly whisk or fork the eggs into a small mixing dish until they are well combined. In a separate bowl, whisk together the milk and thyme.

- Reduce the heat to medium-low and add the egg mixture to the skillet. Cook until the eggs are set.

- Gently and regularly stir the eggs with a rubber spatula for 4 to 5 minutes or until they are frothy and completely cooked.

- Season with freshly ground black pepper and serve immediately.

- After cooking, place these eggs in a blender and mix until smooth, then consume on a pureed diet. Eat them as soon as possible while they are still warm. Consider adding tablespoon of powdered egg whites to the egg and milk combination to boost the protein content of the dish. Mix thoroughly to completely dissolve the egg white powder; you will never know it is there because the taste is unaffected. You may also add cheese to the dish to boost the protein content. When you go to a soft diet or a diet of general consistency, you can use slices of lean ham or deli turkey to keep the protein intake high. Additional seasonings for your eggs include rosemary, chives, and dill, as well as salsa or chili sauce to serve on the side for a kick.

Per serving (1/4 cup): calories: 230 Calories in a serving: 87 6 g of total fat Sodium: 83 milligrams

Carbohydrates in total: 1 g 0 g of sugar 0g of dietary fiber 7 g of protein

Chicken Salad with Parsley that has been seasoned with herbs.

- Many individuals find it difficult to add tasty items to their diets after surgery. They become bored consuming protein drinks, cottage cheese, and yogurt in the first few weeks following the procedure. Even though meat is the most protein-dense of all foods, many people who have had surgery initially avoid eating meat since it is exceedingly full and thick. It will be easier to digest when you serve meat with a wet sauce. Most chicken salads are heavy with high-calorie mayonnaise, but this recipe is filled with herbs, spices, and Greek yogurt, resulting in a creamy and delectable final dish.

- 2 tablespoons plain Greek yogurt (low-fat or nonfat) freshly squeezed lemon juice (around 1 tablespoon) 1 tablespoon onion flakes (dried or fresh)

- 1 teaspoon Dijon mustard (optional)

- 1/4 teaspoon oregano leaves, dried

- 1 / 4 teaspoon ground garlic powder

- Cooked chicken chopped into 1/2 cups or 1 (1/2.5-ounce) can of chicken breast

- peppercorns that have been freshly ground

- 1 / 4 cup finely chopped fresh parsley

- Using a medium-sized mixing bowl, thoroughly blend the yogurt, lemon juice, onion flakes, mustard, oregano, and garlic powder until thoroughly incorporated.

- Sprinkle pepper on top of the chicken and blend until everything is thoroughly incorporated and the chicken is covered in sauce. Add in the parsley and mix well.

- Serve immediately or cover and chill overnight to let the flavors develop more.

Per serving (1/4 cup): calories: 230 84 calories per serving 2 g of total fat Sodium: 43 milligrams Carbohydrates in total: 1 g 0 g of sugar 0g of dietary fiber 16 g of protein

Tuna Salad with Lemon and Dill.

Lemon is almost usually used to season seafood and fish dishes. As the lemon is crucial in eradicating any fish stink while also delivering a sharp pop of fresh flavor, it has been a culinary tradition for hundreds of years. Fish and seafood are high in protein and low in calories, making them excellent additions to any weight-loss diet. Besides being economical, tuna in a can is also highly handy and well-tolerated following surgery. This tuna salad mixes the taste of dill with the brightness of fresh lemon.

- 1 can of tuna packed in water

- lemon juice (about 2 tablespoons) that has been freshly squeezed

- 1 tablespoon mayonnaise (optional)

- one-and-a-half tablespoons of plain Greek yogurt

- 1 teaspoon dried dill (optional)

- 1/2 teaspoon garlic powder (optional)

- 1/2 teaspoon Dijon mustard (optional)

- fresh ground black pepper (about 1/2 teaspoon)

- Drain the tuna through a fine-mesh sieve into a large mixing bowl. Transfer the mixture to a small mixing basin.

- Toss the tuna with lemon juice, mayonnaise, Greek yogurt, dill, garlic powder, mustard, and pepper in a large mixing basin until everything is thoroughly blended.

- Serve immediately or cover and chill overnight to let the flavors develop more.

- Tuna salad may be made in various ways to keep it fresh and interesting. Here are a few extra possibilities: Pickles, finely chopped fresh onion, peas, or sunflower seeds can be included in a general-purpose diet. Replace the mayonnaise with avocado to make the dish extra creamy while increasing the amount of nutritious fat.

Per serving (1/4 cup): calories: 230 82 calories per serving 4 g of total fat Sodium: 240 milligrams Carbohydrates in total: 0g 0 g of sugar 0g of dietary fiber 11 g of protein.

Chapter Three

Breakfast

Slow Cooker Cinnamon Oatmeal is a hearty breakfast dish.

There's a reason oatmeal is such a popular breakfast choice for so many people: it's hearty and nourishing, and it can be completely personalized with any toppings you choose. In addition, oats are nutritious grain high in nutrients, fiber, and even a small amount of protein. Oatmeal may be prepared in various ways, but using a slow cooker is the most convenient and hands-off method. Simply place the ingredients in the machine before bed and set it on in the morning, and your oatmeal will be ready. Due to a large number of ingredients in this recipe, it is simple to split the mixture into little containers to enjoy throughout the week. It's also simple to prepare ahead of time and freeze for later use.

- 8 quarts of water

- Steel-cut oats (about 2 cups)

- ground cinnamon (about 1 to 2 tablespoons)

- Add-ins to increase protein intake (limit to 1 powder to maintain desirable consistency)

- 1/2 cups skim milk or nonfat milk (add before serving or while reheating) Unflavored or vanilla-flavored protein powder (about 2 teaspoons total) 2 tablespoons nonfat powdered milk or egg white powder (or a combination thereof)

- a couple of teaspoons of powdered peanut butter

- Flavorings and seasonings 8+ weeks post-operatively:

- 1/2 cup berries, either fresh or frozen

- 1/2 ounce of peeled and sliced apple, pear, peach, or banana

- Pumpkin puree (1/4 cup)

- 2 tablespoons toasted walnuts or almonds, finely chopped

- Combine the water, oats, and cinnamon in a slow cooker and set aside. Cook on low heat for 7 to 8 hours, covered.

- Before serving, select and combine your favorite flavoring ingredients.

- All year long, oatmeal is a delicious breakfast option, and the diversity of ingredients you choose ensures that your morning routine never becomes stale.

Per Serving (34 cups, no additional ingredients): Calories consumed: 137 2 g of total fat Sodium: 0 milligrams Carbohydrates in total: 23g 0 g of sugar 4 g of dietary fiber 6 g of protein

Pancakes.

Breakfast favorite on the weekends, pancakes are loaded with sweet syrup and butter, causing you to go over your daily sugar and fat allowances in no time. Fortunately, there is a method to make this family favorite in a way that is high in protein while maintaining the cake-like texture that everyone loves. Consume simple, or top with plain yogurt and fresh berries to make a parfait. They're also delicious when served with unsweetened applesauce on top.

- Eggs

- 1 cup cottage cheese (low-fat or nonfat)

- 13 cups whole-wheat pastry flour (optional)

- Canola oil (11 1/2 tablespoons)

- Cooking spray with a nonstick coating

- Lightly whisk the eggs in a large mixing dish.

- Combine the cottage cheese, flour, and canola oil in a small bowl until barely mixed.

- Prepare a big pan or skillet by gently spraying it with cooking spray and heating it over medium heat.

- Pour 13 cups of batter onto the skillet for each pancake, using a measuring cup to ensure even distribution. Allow 2 to 3 minutes for each pancake to cook or until bubbles develop over the surface of each pancake. Cook for 1 to 2 minutes on the other side, or until the pancakes are golden brown, before flipping them over.

- Serve as soon as possible.

Per serving (1 pancake), the following amounts are provided: Calories in this recipe: 182 10 g of total fat 68 milligrams of sodium Carbohydrates in total: 10 g 1 gram of sugar 3 g of dietary fiber 1/2 g of protein

Crustless chicken and cheese quiche.

A filling, protein-packed breakfast like this quiche

is a great way to start the day. Make a quick breakfast using the leftover grilled chicken from yesterday's supper by combining it with other ingredients. Try adding chopped vegetables such as bell peppers, onions, and tomatoes to your dish to sneak in some additional veggies. We've already discussed how quiche isn't limited to morning meals. Make this dish for a weekday dinner, and you'll keep everyone's palates satisfied and their bellies filled.

Cooking spray with a nonstick coating

Cubed grilled, boiled, baked, or canned chicken breast; 4 ounces Swiss cheese; 8 ounces shredded low-fat mozzarella cheese; 6 ounces (11/4 cups) shredded low-fat mozzarella cheese

- 1/2 tsp. dried basil (optional)

- 1/2 teaspoon oregano leaves (dried)

- 1/4 teaspoon thyme leaves (dry) 3 quail eggs

- 1 cup skim milk (or nonfat milk)

- Preheat the oven to 400 degrees Fahrenheit.

- Spray a 9-inch pie pan with nonstick cooking spray and set aside.

- Place the chicken and Swiss cheese on a pie plate and bake for 30 minutes.

- Toss the mozzarella over the top and sprinkle the basil, oregano, and thyme over everything to finish.

- Whisk the eggs and milk until well combined in a medium-sized mixing basin. Pour the egg mixture over the chicken and cheese, and set aside to set.

- For 40 minutes, or until the top is gently browned, bake the cake. Allow the quiche to rest for 5 minutes before cutting and serving it immediately.

- The quiche may be refrigerated for up to 1 week at room temperature. Then, simply reheat the quiche just before serving.

- In terms of omega-3 fatty acids, eggs are a fantastic supply. For some of these heart-healthy and anti-inflammatory fats, choose organic cage-free eggs, fresh farm eggs, or omega-3 fortified eggs to include in your diet.

Per serving (1 slice), the following amounts are provided: Calories in a serving: 186 10 g of total fat

Sodium: 360 milligrams Carbohydrates in total: 4 g 0 g of sugar 0g of dietary fiber 20 g of protein

Incredible Deviled.

It is undoubtedly referred to as the "amazing, edible egg." Eggs are a cheap source of protein, vitamins, and minerals, and they may be used in variouscooking processes. Deviled eggs don't have to be just for Easter brunches any more! They make a delicious breakfast, mid-afternoon snack, or side dish to accompany lunch or supper. The key ingredient in this dish is Dijon mustard, which adds a tangy tang to usually bland-flavored eggs. Take advantage of the short preparation time and nutritional ingredients in deviled eggs as an appetizer!

- Six quail eggs

- 3 tablespoons extra-virgin olive oil mayonnaise

- 1 tbsp Dijon mustard (optional)

- peppercorns that have been freshly ground

- paprika powder, to be used as a garnish

- Over high heat, fill a big saucepan halfway with water and quickly bring it to a vigorous boil.

- Using a spoon, carefully put the eggs in the boiling water and set a timer for 10 minutes to cook the eggs.

- To halt the cooking process, immediately remove the eggs from the boiling water to a colander and pour cold water over the eggs to stop the boiling process.

- Peel the eggs as soon as they have cooled enough to handle.

- Combine the mayonnaise, mustard, and black pepper in a small bowl until well combined.

- Carefully cut each egg in half lengthwise and scoop out the yolks into a mixing bowl with the mayonnaise mixture on the side of the bowl. Combine the yolks and mayonnaise mixture in a large bowl until thoroughly mixed. The consistency of the mixture should be smooth and creamy.

- Place each egg white half, cut-side up, on a plate or serving dish with care so that it does not break. Make a well in the center of each egg half and pour in approximately two teaspoons of the filling mixture (divided evenly among the 1/2 egg halves). Sprinkle each with a pinch of paprika.

- Serve right away or store in the refrigerator for up to 3 days.

- The egg white comprises the bulk of the protein in an egg, but the yolk also includes a small amount of protein and the majority of the other nutrients, such as fat-soluble vitamins, minerals, and choline, found in an egg. Choline is a vitamin that is required for proper brain and liver function. You can save calories by eating only the whites of eggs, but you will get the most nutritious benefit if you consume the complete egg.

Per Serving (1 half of a deviled egg): calorie count: 50 4 g of total fat Sodium: 90 milligrams Carbohydrates in total: 0g 0 g of sugar 0g of dietary fiber 3 g of protein

Egg Casserole.

This egg dish serves many people and may be prepared the night before. Many people find it difficult to consume the necessary daily portions of fruits and vegetables, especially after surgery when they only consume a small amount of food. This is a fantastic way to get some additional vegetables into your diet first thing in the morning. Not feeding a large number of people? It's not an issue. Store the leftovers in tiny containers in the refrigerator to reheat for the next few morning's breakfasts, and freeze the remainder for use later, if desired.

- Cooking spray with a nonstick coating
- Extra-virgin olive oil (about 2 tablespoons)
- 1 teaspoon minced garlic, if desired
- 1/2 ounces chopped red bell pepper

- 1/2 yellow bell pepper, diced 4 ounces (11/2 cups) diced mushrooms 1/2 yellow bell pepper, diced

- 1/2 medium-sized red onions, chopped 1 cup spinach (about)

- a total of 18 eggs

- low-fat milk (about 2 tablespoons)

- 1/2 teaspoon oregano leaves (dried)

- 1/2 tsp. dried basil (optional)

- 1/4 teaspoon red pepper flakes (optional)

- 3 medium tomatoes, peeled and diced

- 3 tablespoons mozzarella cheese (low-fat shredded)

- 1/2 cup shredded Parmesan cheese (optional)

- Preheat the oven to 350 degrees Fahrenheit. Prepare a 9-by-13-inch baking dish by spraying it with cooking spray and placing it aside.

- Heat the olive oil in a large pan over medium heat until shimmering. Sauté the garlic, red and yellow bell peppers, mushrooms, and onion in the heated oil for 3 to 5 minutes or until the vegetables are soft but not mushy.

- Toss in the spinach and simmer for 1 to 2 minutes or until it begins to wilt. Turn off the heat and remove the skillet from the stove.

- In a large mixing bowl, whisk together the eggs, milk, oregano, basil, and red pepper flakes until well combined and smooth.

- Toss in the cooked veggies, tomatoes, and mozzarella to the egg mixture and combine thoroughly. Using a whisk, mix all of the ingredients.

- Pour the mixture into the baking dish and sprinkle the Parmesan cheese on top to finish it.

- Preheat the oven to 350°F and bake for 35-40 minutes or until gently browned. Allow for a 5-minute resting period before serving the dish.

- You may keep leftovers in the refrigerator for up to 1 week if you plan. Then, before serving, reheat the dish.

- Make this egg casserole your own and make it more intriguing by including different ingredients to change the filling. Cooked spicy turkey or chicken sausage is a good option. Think about topping it with sliced avocado and Fresh

Salsa or spicy sauce to amp up the flavor even more.

Serving Size (in ounces): Calories in a serving: 133 8 g of total fat 172 milligrams of sodium Carbohydrates in total: 3 g 1 gram of sugar 0g of dietary fiber 11 g of protein

Breakfast in bed: Mini Egg Muffins with Turkey Bacon.

Like the convenience of a grab-and-go breakfast but don't want to go to a drive-through restaurant? These little egg muffins with flavorful turkey bacon will leave you feeling full, yet they have far less fat and salt than traditional egg muffins. The nicest aspect is that you can prepare a large quantity and store it in the freezer during the week or month.

You may experiment with other ingredients like spinach, mushrooms, sliced bell peppers, onions, or other favorite omelet components.

- Cooking spray with a nonstick coating
- 1/2 slice of fried turkey bacon, quartered between each piece 1/2 big quail eggs
- a quarter-cup of low-fat milk
- 1/2 teaspoon oregano leaves (dried)
- 1/2 teaspoons dried basil 1/4 teaspoon freshly ground black pepper 1/2 teaspoon dried basil 1/4 teaspoon freshly ground black pepper
- 1/4 teaspoon ground garlic powder
- 1-1/2 cups finely grated Swiss or Monterey Jack cheese, split

- Preheat the oven to 350 degrees Fahrenheit. Cooking sprays a 24-cup mini muffin tray with a nonstick coating.

- Placing 2 turkey bacon bits in the bottom of each muffin cup will make them more filling.

- Using an electric mixer on medium speed, beat the eggs and milk until combined. Add the oregano, basil, pepper, and garlic powder and whisk until combined. Add 34 cups of the cheese and mix well.

- Fill each muffin cup three-quarters of the way with the egg mixture and bake for 20 minutes. On top of the muffins, sprinkle with the remaining 1/4 cup of cheese.

- Place the baking sheet in the oven for 20 to 25 minutes or until the eggs are set. Allow for around 2 minutes of cooling time before serving the muffins.

- Refrigerate for up to 1 week or freeze for up to 1 month after making the dressing.

- Eggs have a negative reputation due to the yolk's significant amount of dietary cholesterol. However, a study found that consuming eggs as part of a well-balanced diet with plenty of fiber and little saturated fat had no negative influence on blood cholesterol levels. Bottom line: Eat your eggs without feeling guilty, and restrict your intake of other foods high in saturated fats to maintain a heart-healthy diet.

Per serving (2 small egg muffins), the following amounts are provided: Calories in a serving: 153 8 g of total fat Sodium: 232 milligrams Carbohydrates in total: 8 g 1 gram of sugar 1 gram of fiber 13 g of protein

Overnight Bircher Muesli

Do you enjoy the warm and nourishing qualities of hot oatmeal but despise that it is too hot to consume during summer? To put a new spin on cold oats, try this recipe. Whether you're satisfied from the bottom of your spirit to the top of your stomach, you'll wake up feeling rejuvenated even on the hottest days. In addition, you won't have to turn on the burner or use the microwave. Try it at any time of the year!

- 2 cups rolled oats (the old-fashioned kind)
- 1 cup skim milk (or nonfat milk)

- 1 cup plain Greek yogurt with no added sugar

- 1 teaspoon ground cinnamon 1 tablespoon honey 1 teaspoon ground cinnamon

- 1/2 teaspoons of pure vanilla essence

- Add-ins for protein (limit to one tablespoon per serving to maintain desired consistency) teaspoons protein powder, unflavored or vanilla flavored

- 2 tablespoons nonfat powdered milk or egg white powder (or a combination thereof)

- Peanut butter powder (about 2 teaspoons)

- Additional add-ons 8 to 10 weeks post-operatively (choose 1 or more)

- cup of berries (fresh or frozen)

- teaspoon ground flaxseed 1 apple, peeled and diced

- chia seeds (about 2 teaspoons)

- 2 tablespoons almonds, slivered or finely chopped

- In a large container that can be firmly covered, combine the oats, milk, yogurt, honey, cinnamon, and vanilla until well combined. Add in the seasonings of your choosing and mix well.

- Wrap it tightly and place it in the refrigerator overnight to enable the flavors to mingle and the oats to soften.

- Keep refrigerated and consume within 1 week of preparation.

- You may prepare it ahead of time and freeze individual servings to enjoy throughout the week. Gather a few small reusable plastic containers with lids and place individual portions in each container on the first morning of the month. Then, store it in the refrigerator to make a quick grab-and-go meal for the entire family.

Per serving (about 34 cups): Calories: 242 per serving 4 g of total fat Sodium: 67 milligrams Carbohydrates in total: 38g 9 g of sugar 4 g of dietary fiber 13 g of protein

Smoked Salmon Breakfast Toast.

Making these smoked salmon toasts couldn't be much simpler, and they're filled with nutritional value. I propose avoiding the traditional bagel and lox, which contains high-fat and low-protein cream cheese and replacing it with avocado to increase your intake of heart-healthy fat and protein. In addition, avocado's soothing smoothness, which is gently melted over the bread while it's still warm, along with salmon's saltiness, makes for a delicious and healthful combo.

- 2 tablespoons plain Greek yogurt (low-fat or nonfat)

- 1/2 ounces of freshly squeezed lemon juice

- 1 ripe avocado

- 4 slices whole-grain bread with sprouted grains (100 percent whole-grain)

- 8 ounces smoked salmon (optional)

- 2 sprigs of fresh dill

- Whisk together the yogurt and lemon juice in a small bowl until well combined.

- Cut the avocado in half, remove the pit, and scoop the flesh into a mixing dish with the yogurt and salt. Make a thorough mix. The avocado mixture should be rather smooth, with no huge bits of avocado visible in the final product.

- Toast the bread until it is golden brown.

- Each bread piece should be layered with the avocado mixture and 2 ounces of smoked salmon, with fresh dill sprinkled on top of each. Serve as soon as possible.

- Fish high in omega-3 fatty acids, such as salmon, mackerel, and tuna, should be consumed at least twice a week, according to the American Heart Association, for optimal heart health. Healthy fats found in fatty fish, such as omega-3 fatty acids, can help to lower cholesterol and reduce the risk of heart disease and stroke.

Per serving (1 toast), the following amounts are provided: Calories in 1 serving: 231 10 g of total fat Sodium: 646 milligrams Carbohydrates in total: 19g 2 g of sugar 6 g of dietary fiber 18 g of protein

Muffins with blueberries.

You might be missing your usual fluffy, bakery-fresh blueberry muffins, which melt in your mouth but are laden with sugar, so try these instead. Enjoy this tasty muffin that will satisfy your taste senses while helping you meet your daily protein requirements. Typical sweet blueberry muffins provide an initial burst of energy followed by a subsequent crash, leaving you needing more. These delectable baked treats will satisfy your sweet need without causing you to crash and burn from too much sugar.

- 3 / 4 cup unflavored protein powder 1 1/2 cups whole-wheat pastry flour
- 2 tablespoons toasted flaxseed (ground)
- baking powder (11 1/2 teaspoons)
- 1 teaspoon of cinnamon, ground
- 1/2 teaspoon bicarbonate of soda
- applesauce (without added sugar) - 1 cup
- 1/2 cup plain Greek yogurt with no added sugar
- honey (about 2 teaspoons)
- 1 teaspoon pure vanilla extract (optional)

- freshly grated lemon zest (about 1 teaspoon)

- 3 egg whites (optional)

- 1 cup fresh or frozen blueberries, thawed and mashed

- Preheat the oven to 350 degrees Fahrenheit. Make a 1/2-cup muffin tray by lining it with paper liners and setting it aside.

- In a medium-sized mixing bowl, combine the flour, protein powder, flaxseed, baking powder, cinnamon, and baking soda until thoroughly combined.

- Combine the applesauce, yogurt, honey, vanilla, and lemon zest in a large mixing bowl until well combined. Gradually include the egg whites until everything is just blended.

- Toss in the flour mixture until it barely incorporates the wet ingredients. Next, add the blueberries and gently mix them in.

- Fill the muffin cups three-quarters of the way with the batter and bake for 20 minutes.

- Baking time is 10 to 15 minutes, or until a toothpick inserted into the center of a muffin emerges clean.

- Before serving the muffins, remove the muffin tray from the oven and place it on a wire rack to cool.

Per serving (1 muffin), the following amounts are provided: Calories in this recipe: 181 1 gram of total fat Sodium: 163 milligrams Carbohydrates in total: 32 g 8 g of sugar 5 g of fiber 1/2 g of protein

Breakfast Burritos with Turkey.

Breakfast burritos at a gas station on the way to work are a thing of the past, and you should be grateful. But, on the other hand, a savory breakfast sandwich is not off the menu. Even while these breakfast burritos are filled with fluffy eggs and tasty sausage, they don't include any extra salt and fat. Simply prepare them ahead of time and freeze them before heating them for a nice breakfast in minutes.

- 1/2 hen's eggs

- 1 / 4 cup of nonfat milk

- 1 pound turkey breakfast sausage that is exceptionally lean (nitrate-free)

- Cooking spray with a nonstick coating

- 8 whole-wheat tortillas (7 to 8 inches in diameter), such as La Tortilla Factory low-carb tortillas

- Salsa Verde (fresh salsa)

- Optional add-ons

- 1/4 cup sautéed onion, bell peppers, spinach, and/or mushrooms (optional).

- 1/4 cup refried black beans

- 2 tablespoons shredded cheese of your preference 2 slices of turkey bacon, finely chopped

- Whisk the eggs and milk until well combined in a large mixing basin.

- Cook the turkey sausage in a large pan over medium-high heat for about 7 minutes or until it is well-cooked and no longer pink in the middle. Place the sausage in a large mixing dish and set aside.

- Use a paper towel to wipe out the pan, or use a big skillet sprayed with cooking spray and placed over medium-low heat to finish cleaning. For 10 to 15 minutes, using a rubber spatula, gently and continually whisk the egg mixture until it is frothy and well-cooked.

- Distribute the sausage and scrambled eggs among the tortillas in a circular pattern. If you're using any optional ingredients, put them in the tortilla immediately. Then fold the end of the tortilla, tuck in the edges, and roll it securely to seal it.

- Make ahead and store in a zip-top bag in the refrigerator for up to 1 week, or serve immediately with the salsa. To consume, warm a tortilla in the microwave for 60 to 90 seconds on high on low. Alternatively, they would store nicely in the freezer for up to one month.

- It's possible to make a hundred distinct variations of these breakfast burritos. For example, cook various veggies and combine them in the dish, or use vegetarian proteins such as soy crumbles or other beans to vary the flavor profile. It will keep your taste senses intrigued, and you will stay away from greasy fast-food burritos that will leave you less than satisfied if the ingredients are changed.

Per Serving (1 tortilla with no additional toppings): Calories consumed: 241 10 g of total fat Sodium: 743 milligrams Carbohydrates in total: 27g 1 gram of sugar 7 g of dietary fiber 20 g of protein

Chapter Four

Side Meals

Roasted Tomatoes, Peppers, and Zucchini with Italian Herbs.

The majority of the population dislikes vegetables. Roasted veggies are my preferred method of consuming vegetables. By roasting any veggies in the oven, you can bring out their inherent sweet flavor and a slew of additional tastes you didn't even realize were available from something so straightforward. Cook up some of these roasted veggies for dinner today, and you'll suddenly become a vegetable enthusiast.

- Cooking spray with a nonstick coating 1 medium zucchini (about)

- 2 big tomatoes or 2 cups cherry tomatoes (depending on size)

- 2 red, green, yellow, or orange bell peppers, or a combination of two types of peppers 2 tbsp. Extra-virgin olive oil (optional).

- 1 teaspoon minced garlic, if desired

- 1 teaspoon oregano leaves (dried)

- 1 teaspoon dried basil (optional)

- 1/2 teaspoon thyme leaves (dry)

- 1/2 teaspoons of rosemary (dry)

- Preheat the oven to 425 degrees Fahrenheit. Cooking spray should be sprayed over a large baking sheet with a rim.

- To prepare the veggies, snip off the ends of the zucchini and then cut it in half lengthwise, then cut it into thin slices lengthwise again. Next, using a sharp knife, cut off the ends and cores of the tomatoes, then cut them into 2-inch chunks; if using cherry tomatoes, split them in half. Next, remove the stems from the bell peppers and cut them in half lengthwise; removing the seeds and ribs and chopping them into 1-inch chunks is a good way to start.

- Organize the veggies on a baking sheet and drizzle them with olive oil, garlic, oregano, basil, thyme, and rosemary, then bake for 30 minutes. Using a spoon, thoroughly combine the veggies and spices.

- Roast for 20 to 25 minutes, tossing halfway through or until all of the veggies are cooked, depending on the size of your oven.

- Serve as soon as possible.

- Replace the veggies in this recipe with whichever vegetables are in season at the preparation time. For example, to roast a whole head of cabbage, quarter it and drizzle it with olive oil before firmly wrapping it in aluminum foil and baking it for 45 minutes;grilling it on the grill is a simple and delicious method.

Per 1/2-cup serving (approximately): Calories in one serving: 47 3 g of total fat Sodium: 5 milligrams Carbohydrates in total: 4 g 2 g of sugar 1 gram of fiber 1 gram of protein

Roasted Rosemary

Even though French fries are a mainstay in the average American diet, their salty flavor is a source of comfort for many individuals. Greasy fried food is off-limits after bariatric surgery, not just because it is high in fat and calories but also because it might make you feel ill if consumed too frequently. However, this does not rule out the possibility of preparing a healthy version of this side dish. These savory and sweet potato wedges are a delicious combination. Cooking them for a longer period makes them crunchier. So go ahead and indulge in your next side of fries guilt-free!

- 4 medium sweet potatoes (about 1 1/2 pounds) peeled and diced

- 6 garlic cloves (optional)

- 2 tbsp apple cider vinegar (optional)

- 2 tbsp. Extra-virgin olive oil (optional).

- 1 tablespoon fresh rosemary, finely chopped

- 2 to 3 sprigs of fresh rosemary, chopped

- Preheat the oven to 425 degrees Fahrenheit. Prepare a big baking sheet with a rim by lining it with aluminum foil and setting it aside.

- Make 8 wedges of each sweet potato by halving it lengthwise and slicing each piece lengthwise until you have approximately 8 wedges per sweet potato.

- Put all ingredients in a large mixing basin, except the chopped rosemary, and stir well to combine. Add the potato wedges to the bowl and toss to evenly coat with the dressing.

- Transfer the sweet potatoes and spices to a baking sheet, keeping the garlic cloves intact, and arrange the rosemary sprigs on top of the potato wedges. Bake for 30 minutes or until the potatoes are tender.

- Roast the sweet potatoes for 35 minutes, tossing them every 10 minutes to prevent them from scorching. When the edges of the potatoes get crispy and begin to brown, the potatoes are done.

- Serve as soon as possible.

Per serving (4 wedges), the following amounts are provided: Calories in a serving: 103 3 g of total fat Sodium: 47 milligrams Carbohydrates in total: 18g 4 g of sugar 3 g of dietary fiber 1 gram of protein

Cucumber Salad with Asian Flavors.

This cold and refreshing cucumber salad is the perfect way to counteract a spicy lunch. In addition, it's a great option for creamy coleslaws and salads that are rich in calories and fat, such as those found in fast food restaurants. This recipe will stay in the refrigerator for about a week, so be sure to put any leftovers in an airtight container and eat it throughout the week.

- 3 medium cucumbers, cleaned and cut at the ends before being thinly sliced (about 4 cups)
- 2 scallions, cut into white and green sections
- 1/4 cup sliced red onion (optional)
- 1/4 cup chopped red bell pepper (optional)
- 1/4 cup rice wine vinegar (optional)
- sesame seeds (about 2 tablespoons)
- 1 tbsp. honey (optional)

- 1/2 teaspoon sesame oil (optional)

- one-and-a-half teaspoons of salt

- 1/4 teaspoon red pepper flakes (optional)

- Mix the cucumbers, scallions, red onion, and bell pepper in a medium-sized mixing basin until well-combined.

- In a small mixing bowl, whisk together the vinegar, sesame seeds, honey, sesame oil, salt, and red pepper flakes until well combined and smooth.

- Mix in the dressing slowly until everything is well-combined after pouring it over the veggies.

- Refrigerate for at least 30 minutes before serving to allow flavors to blend.

Per 1/2-cup serving (approximately): Calories in a serving: 45 1 gram of total fat Sodium: 368

milligrams Carbohydrates in total: 8 g 5 g of sugar 1 gram of fiber 1 gram of protein

Ratatouille over Spaghetti Squash.

You crave spaghetti but don't want to consume too many calories and carbohydrates. As a bonus, you don't want to leave the dinner feeling like you've swallowed an overinflated balloon. Starchy meals tend to make most people feel overstuffed and uncomfortable after surgery. Spaghetti squash is a delicious substitute for pasta with only one-fifth of the calories in traditional pasta. Use your abundant summer veggies to make ratatouille instead of store-bought spaghetti sauce, which is typically rich in sugar and missing a variety of vegetables. Step further by adding cheese, turkey sausage, or roasted chicken to increase the amount of protein in your meal.

- Cooking spray with a nonstick coating
- 1/4 cup extra-virgin olive oil 1 small (3- to 4-pound) spaghetti squash 1 tablespoon minced garlic
- 1 teaspoon minced garlic, if desired
- 1 medium yellow onion, chopped (about)
- 2 cups chopped yellow and orange bell peppers
- 1/4 cup finely chopped fresh basil
- 1/4 cup finely chopped fresh parsley
- 1 teaspoon thyme leaves (dried)
- 1/4 teaspoon fresh rosemary

- 1 medium eggplant, sliced into 1/2-inch pieces with the peel still on

- 1 medium zucchini, thinly sliced into 1/2-inch rounds

- 1 medium yellow squash, peeled and sliced into 1/2-inch pieces

- Tomatoes: 1 1/2 cups, seeded and sliced into 1/4-inch dice

- Preheat the oven to 375 degrees Fahrenheit. Prepare a baking sheet with a rim by spraying it with cooking spray and setting it aside.

- Cut the spaghetti squash in half lengthwise and scoop out the seeds.

- Place the squash on a baking sheet with the sliced side facing up. Roast the squash for approximately 40 minutes or until it is fork-tender.

- While the squash is roasting, heat the olive oil in a large pan over medium heat until shimmering. Toss in the garlic and cook for approximately 30 seconds or until it becomes aromatic. Combine the onion and bell pepper in a large mixing bowl. Cook the veggies for approximately 5 minutes or until they are soft. Combine the basil, parsley, thyme, and rosemary in a large mixing bowl until everything is thoroughly blended.

- Add the eggplant, zucchini, and yellow squash to the skillet and cook for about 10 minutes, until the vegetables are soft. Cook for another 10 minutes or until all of the veggies is soft, after which you may remove them from the heat. Make a mental note to put it away.

- To remove the flesh from the squash, wait until it has cooled enough to handle before scraping it with a fork. The squash should naturally separate into spaghetti-like strands when cut in half lengthwise.

- Combine the squash noodles and the ratatouille mixture in a serving dish.

- If you get a bigger spaghetti squash, you can create a significant quantity of "noodles," which you can reheat and serve throughout the week with various toppings.

Per 1/2-cup serving (approximately): Calories in one serving: 136 8 g of total fat Sodium: 13 milligrams Carbohydrates in total: 1/4g 5 g of sugar 6 g of dietary fiber 2 g of protein

Roasted Chickpeas with a Crunchy Crunch.

Many patients find it difficult to refrain from mindless munching following surgery. For many patients I have dealt with, grazing or nibbling on food throughout the day has long been a habit. Unfortunately, snacking is a convenient method to consume excessive calories, and the majority of the items we consume as snacks—potato chips, pretzels, cookies—are poor in nutritional content and heavy in calories, allowing us to consume a significant quantity before our gut realizes that we are satisfied. Try to keep snacking to a bare minimum, but here's a healthy alternative that will satisfy your want for something crunchy. Roasting these little beans transforms them from a bland and flavorless beans into something delicious and aromatic.

- Cooking spray that is not a stock item

- 1 chickpea can (15.5 ounces) drained

- 1 tablespoon extra-virgin olive oil (optional)

- 1 teaspoon garlic powder (optional)

- 1 teaspoon onion powder (optional)

- 1/2 teaspoon cayenne pepper, freshly ground

- Preheat the oven to 400 degrees Fahrenheit. Prepare a big-rimmed baking sheet by spraying it with cooking spray and setting it aside.

- Drain and rinse the chickpeas in a colander or sieve until they are no longer sticky.

- In a medium-sized mixing bowl, combine the chickpeas, olive oil, garlic powder, onion powder, and cayenne pepper until well combined.

- On a baking sheet, spread the chickpeas in a single layer to prevent them from sticking. Allow 15 to 20 minutes of roasting time, stirring the vegetables at least once halfway through the cooking period. They are ready to serve when the chickpeas are gently cooked and crispy.

- Serve as soon as possible.

- Eat these crispy chickpeas or sprinkle them into a salad to add flavor, fiber, and protein to your meal.

Per serving (13 cups): calories are as follows: Calories in a serving: 118 2 g of total fat Sodium:

330 milligrams Carbohydrates in total: 20 g 0 g of sugar 5 g of dietary fiber 5 g of protein

Crock Pickles.

- One strategy is to include items that appeal to a wide range of tastes. For example, pickles have a sharp, tangy, and delicious flavor and nearly no calories. Here's a simple recipe far superior to any jarred pickle you've ever had. If feasible, get freshly pickled cucumbers from a farmers' market or grow them in your yard. Because these crunchy pickles do not contain any protein, you should hold off on trying them until you have progressed to the general foods stage of your diet and can satisfy your protein requirements satisfactorily.

- 61 and a half glasses of water

- 1/4 cup canning salt 2 cups distilled white vinegar 2 cups distilled white vinegar

- 4 sprigs of fresh dill

- 3 garlic cloves (optional)

- 10 to 15 pickling cucumbers (about)

- Bring the water, vinegar, and salt to a boil in a large saucepan over high heat, stirring constantly. When the liquid comes to a vigorous boil, remove it from the heat and set it aside to cool for 10 minutes before using it.

- Fill a gallon-size glass jar with a tight-fitting lid and place the dill sprigs, garlic cloves, and pickled cucumbers. Set aside.

- The brine mixture should be poured over the cucumbers so they are thoroughly submerged in the liquid. Then, with the lid on the jar, make a secure seal.

- Allow the pickles to sit on the counter for 3 to 5 days before eating them. The pickles are now ready to consume or can be refrigerated if they have not already been done so. They will last for up to 2 months when stored in the refrigerator.

- Yogurt isn't the only meal that contains probiotics that are beneficial to the gut. Fortunately, because fresh sauerkraut and—you guessed it—pickles are also fermented foods, they contain beneficial bacteria that help keep your gastrointestinal system regular.

Per Pickle (1 Pickle Serving): 9 calories per serving, 0 g of total fat Sodium: 961 milligrams Carbohydrates total: 2g 0 g of sugar 0g of dietary fiber 0 g of protein

Mashed Cauliflower.

Even though potatoes are a staple grain on many families' dinner plates, some people discover that potatoes make their pouch feel excessively full after having weight-loss surgery. Not to add that potatoes have a high carbohydrate and calorie content compared to most other vegetables.

Although potatoes in and of themselves are not particularly harmful to our health, everything we like to add to the—sour cream, butter, bacon bits, and cheese—raises the calorie count significantly. So try this creamy cauliflower substitute instead of mashed potatoes. As a result, it's exceptionally low in calories and carbs while delivering the same creamy texture as your typical mashed potatoes.

- 1 huge head of cauliflower (about)

- 1/4 cup of water

- 13 cups low-fat buttermilk (optional) (or see step 2 to make homemade buttermilk) 1 tablespoon minced garlic, if desired

- olive oil (extra virgin) (about 1 tablespoon)

- Make tiny cauliflower florets and place them in a big microwave-safe basin with water. Microwave for 2 minutes on high. Cover the cauliflower with plastic wrap and microwave for about 5 minutes or until it is tender. Discard any remaining liquid in the dish.

- Buttermilk may be purchased at most supermarkets, but creating your own at home is just as simple. Using 1 teaspoon of freshly squeezed lemon juice and 13 cups of low-fat milk, you may produce your homemade buttermilk! Allow the mixture to rest for approximately 10 minutes or until the milk thickens.

- Process the buttermilk, cauliflower, garlic, and olive oil on medium speed in a blender or food processor until the cauliflower is smooth and creamy.

- Serve as soon as possible.

- To make the cauliflower more flavorful, microwave it with chicken or vegetable broth instead of water, then purée the mixture with 1/2 cup grated Parmesan cheese once it has been blended. When making this vegetable-based dish, you may boost the protein content by including powdered egg whites or unflavored protein powder after the first purée.

Per 1/2-cup serving (approximately): Calories in one serving: 62 2 g of total fat Sodium: 54 milligrams Carbohydrates in total: 8 g 3 g of sugar 3 g of dietary fiber 3 g of protein

Hummus with Roasted Red Peppers

Most of us enjoy adding flavor to our meals with ranch dressing, mayonnaise, catsup, and butter. However, many of these condiments are high in calories and fat, which are undesirable after surgery and should be avoided if possible. Hummus can substitute for mayonnaise on top of burgers, rolled in lunch meat, or as a dip for raw veggies. Because this hummus is so flavorful, you can dispense with the need for additional sauces and cheese. Not to mention, it contains fresh peppers, which are high in vitamin C, which helps to strengthen the immune system.

- Cooking spray with a nonstick coating

- Cut two red bell peppers in thirds, remove the seeds and ribs, and slice each quarter into three pieces.

- 1 (15.5-ounce) can of chickpeas, drained and rinsed

- Juice of 1 lemon

- 1 tablespoon minced garlic, if desired

- 3 tablespoons extra-virgin olive oil

- 2 tablespoons water, plus an additional 1 to 2 tablespoons if needed

- 1/2 teaspoon cumin seeds, ground

- 1/4 teaspoon oregano leaves, dried

- 1 / 4 teaspoon of salt

- Preheat the oven to the broil setting. Prepare a large baking sheet by spraying it with cooking spray and setting it aside.

- Prepare a baking sheet by placing each pepper slice on it with the interior section facing down. Broil the peppers for about 7 minutes, until the skin is browned and the peppers are soft and juicy. Remove from the oven and leave aside to cool.

- On high speed, puree the chickpeas with the lemon juice and garlic until very smooth (about 2 to 3 minutes), then add the olive oil, water, cumin, oregano,salt, and puree until very smooth again (about 2 minutes).

- As soon as the peppers have cooled enough to handle, carefully peel away the charred section of the skin and set it aside. The skin should be easy to pull away.

- Cut the roasted peppers into chunks and place the pieces in a food processor. Process until smooth. To decorate the completed hummus, you may put aside a little quantity to mince and use as a garnish on top of the final product.

- Place the peppers in a food processor with the rest of the ingredients and purée. If extra water is required to get the correct consistency, add 1 to 2 tablespoons until it is reached.

- Serve immediately or refrigerate for up to 1 week in an airtight jar before serving.

Per serving (2 tablespoons), there are the following nutrients: 71 calories per serving, 3 g of total fat Sodium: 136 milligrams Carbohydrates in total: 9g 1 gram of sugar 2 g of dietary fiber, 2 g of protein

Dip in a Mediterranean Style.

Eating this creamy dip bursting with flavor makes you think you're eating all the toppings from a freshly made gyro sandwich. If you bring this to your next office potluck, you will amaze your coworkers with a nutritious and tasty dip that is fewer in calories and richer in nutrients than the traditional spreads. If you have leftovers, you can dress up a simple chicken breast by spreading them on top.

- 10 ounces plain or garlic hummus or hummus with garlic Hummus with Roasted Red Peppers

- 1 tomato, peeled and sliced

- 1/2 cup finely sliced cucumber

- 1/2 cup plain Greek yogurt with no added sugar

- 1/2 lemon, seeded 1/4 teaspoon paprika powder

- 1 (1/4.5-ounce) can artichoke hearts, drained, washed, and cut into 1/4-inch pieces 1 (1/4.5-ounce) can water-packed artichoke hearts, drained, rinsed, and cut into 1/4-inch pieces

- 13/4 cup feta cheese crumbles 1/2 medium red onion, finely chopped

- 1 cup pitted and coarsely chopped Kalamata olives (optional) 2 tablespoons fresh parsley, finely chopped

- Distribute the hummus equally on the bottom of an 8-by-8-inch square baking dish. Place the tomato and cucumber on top of the hummus and spread evenly.

- Spread the yogurt over the veggies with a rubber spatula to ensure it is equally distributed. Squeeze the juice of the lemon over the yogurt and stir to incorporate. Paprika should be sprinkled on top.

- Over the yogurt, arrange the chopped artichokes, red onion, and feta cheese in a layer. Finish with the olives and parsley, if desired.

- Fresh veggies, whole-grain crackers, or whole-grain pita chips are all excellent accompaniments to this dip.

Per serving (1/4 cup): calories: 230 Calories in a serving: 93 5 g of total fat Sodium: 381 milligrams Carbohydrates in total: 8 g 0 g of sugar 2 g of dietary fiber 4 g of protein

Spinach and Artichoke Dip – a delicious appetizer.

Are you looking for an appetizer for your next football party or holiday gathering? Look no further. Look no farther than this spinach-artichoke dip for a delicious appetizer. It has the same creamy, cheesy feel as your favorite dip from your favorite pub or restaurant but without the added fat and calories of the traditional version. Make no apprehensions about the hidden component, tofu. You and your visitors will be completely unaware that it is blended inside. It is essential for the addition of protein, the reduction of calories per serving, and the creation of the ultra-creamy texture of this dip.

- 8 ounces shredded Parmesan cheese, preferably fresh

- 1 tablespoon spicy sauce (optional)

- silken tofu (about 8 ounces)

- 2 cups of freshly chopped spinach (about 2 handfuls)

- 16 ounces plain Greek yogurt with no added sugar

- minced garlic (about 2 tablespoons)

- 1 teaspoon seasoning salt (optional)

- Prepare the artichokes by chopping them into tiny pieces. Try using a clean pair of kitchen scissors to chop them into little pieces.

- Mix everything in a large bowl with a hand mixer on low speed until everything is thoroughly incorporated (about 2 to 3 minutes). Add the artichokes and toss with the mozzarella and Parmesan cheeses, spicy sauce, spinach, yogurt, garlic, and salt.

- Before serving, heat the dip on the stovetop, in the microwave, or a slow cooker until the cheese has melted and the spinach has wilted, about 3 to 5 minutes for each serving. The time required can vary based on how you cook the sauce.

- With fresh veggies or whole-grain crackers, this dish is perfect for sharing.

- This dip produces a large batch—enough to feed a large group of people. Conserve the leftovers and use them to pour over raw chicken breasts before roasting them in the oven to create a delectable spinach-artichoke chicken meal.

Per serving (1/4 cup): calories: 230 Calories in a serving: 139 7 g of total fat Sodium: 551 milligrams Carbohydrates in total: 6g 2 g of sugar 1 gram of fiber 13 g of protein

Dip in a Greek Ranch Sauce.

This creamy ranch dip will brighten up any fresh veggies or salad you like. Grilled or baked chicken breasts also make excellent dippers since the dip imparts a delicious taste while keeping the chicken juicy. Try combining the dip with a can of tuna for a unique take on the conventional tuna salad recipe. No matter how tightly you monitor your protein intake while limiting fat and sugar intake to a minimum, you can't get around the reality that vegetables and lean meats are essential components of your post-operative diet. This simple dip is a delightful and semi-indulgent approach to ensure that we consume nature's healthiest foods, which may not be the most palatable on their own, while also ensuring that we eat enough of them.

- The equivalent of 2 tablespoons of Ranch Seasoning is a type of seasoning used to season meats and vegetables.

- 16 ounces plain Greek yogurt with no added sugar

- In a small bowl, combine the ranch seasoning and the yogurt until well combined. To bring out the full taste of the dip, it should be refrigerated overnight or for at least 30 minutes before serving.

- Pour in some tuna or chicken before mixing to boost the protein and taste of the dip if you're making it during the puree stage.

Per serving (1/4 cup): calories: 230 Calories in one serving: 25 1 gram of total fat Sodium: 1/4 milligrams Carbohydrates in total: 0g 0 g of sugar 0g of dietary fiber 3 g of protein

Baked Beans.

Baked beans are a popular side dish, but the conventional versions are filled with sugar and fried bacon fat, making them unhealthy to consume. This dish is healthier and tastier than any canned version you'll find at your local grocery store or restaurant. It needs a day of preparation due to the requirement to soak the beans overnight; however, it only takes around 10 minutes to put together because you probably already have most of the basic components in your cupboard.

- pinto beans (dry) weighing 1/2 pound

- 1 can (15 ounces) tomato sauce (optional)
1 and a third cups of water

- 1 cup low-sodium soy sauce or Bragg Liquid Aminos (optional)

- 2 tbsp apple cider vinegar (optional)

- 1 tablespoon molasses (optional)

- 1 tablespoon cumin seeds, ground

- minced garlic (about 2 tablespoons)

- Chili Powder (11 1/2 teaspoons)

- 1/2 teaspoon onion powder (optional)

- 1 / 4 teaspoon ground dry mustard powder

- 1 / 4 teaspoon of salt

- Fill a medium-sized mixing basin with enough cold water to cover the beans by at least 2 inches. Cover with plastic wrap, place in the refrigerator, and soak overnight.

- Drain and rinse the beans in a colander or sieve to remove any remaining debris.

- Combine the beans, tomato sauce, water, soy sauce, vinegar, molasses, cumin, garlic, chili powder, onion powder, mustard powder, and salt in a slow cooker until the beans are tender. Cook the beans on low heat for 7 to 8 hours, covered in the slow cooker, until tender. When the sauce has thickened,and the beans are tender, the beans are ready to be served.

- Turn the slow cooker's temperature to warm and let it aside for 30 minutes before serving the baked beans to soak up the flavors.

- Beans are a great source of soluble fiber, which is important for digestive health. In addition, the presence of soluble fiber is beneficial for heart health because it aids in the removal of cholesterol from the body. Therefore, consume one or two servings of beans or legumes in your diet weekly to help control your blood cholesterol levels.

Per 1/2-cup serving (approximately): 136 calories, 0 grams of fat, total Sodium: 606 milligrams, 26 g of carbohydrates in total, 5 g of sugar, 6 g of dietary fiber, 8 g of protein.

Chapter Five

Dinner

Zucchini Boats Stuffed with Ground Beef and Cheese.

Here are all your favorite Italian dishes condensed into a single dish: lean ground beef, mozzarella cheese, Italian spices, and tomatoes—all without the hefty carbohydrate load of pasta. If you have a large zucchini harvest from your garden, this is a fantastic way to use it.

- 4 medium zucchini (about)

- Cooking spray with a nonstick coating

- 1 pound extra-lean ground beef 1 pound ground turkey

- 1/2 cup finely chopped onion 1 egg that has been gently beaten

- mushroom slices (about 1/2 pounds)

- 1 big tomato, peeled and sliced

- 1 (8-ounce) can of tomato sauce (or similar)

- 1/4 cup bread crumbs made from whole wheat

- 1/2 teaspoon oregano leaves (dried)

- 1/2 tsp. dried basil (optional)

- 1/4 teaspoon freshly ground black pepper, freshly ground

- 1 cup shredded low-fat mozzarella cheese, sliced into quarters

- Preheat the oven to 350 degrees Fahrenheit.

- Remove the zucchini's ends and cut them in half lengthwise to make halves.

- For the zucchini halves to lie flat, a tiny edge should be cut from the rounded side of each half. Scoop out the pulp, leaving shells that are 1/4 inches broad. Remove the pulp from the pan.

- Place the boats in a dish that can be used in the microwave and the oven, and fill the dish with approximately 1 1/4 cup of water at the bottom. Heat in the microwave on high for 3 minutes, or until the boats are crisp-tender, covering the dish with a lid or plastic wrap. Using a strainer, remove the liquid from the dish and set it aside.

- Cooking sprays a big pan and heat it over medium heat until it is hot but not smoking. Allow 7 minutes to elapse between the ground beef and onion being cooked until the meat is no longer pink and the onion is soft. Remove the skillet from the heat and set it aside to drain any remaining fat.

- Put the ingredients in a big mixing bowl and combine them thoroughly. Combine the zucchini pulp with the egg, the mushrooms with the diced tomatoes with the tomato sauce, and the bread crumbs with the oregano basil pepper, ground beef, and onion combination.

- Fill each zucchini boat with approximately 1 1/4 cup of the mixture.

- Sprinkle the remaining 1/2 cup of cheese over the tops of the rolls.

- Bake for 20 minutes, uncovered, or until the cheese is melted and gently browned, then remove from the oven and serve.

- Constipation is a common complaint among people who have had bariatric surgery. There might be a variety of causes for a decrease in the frequency of bowel movements, but one of the most common is that people are consuming less fiber. Many patients are concerned about adopting a low-carb diet because they believe that grains are the primary source of fiber in their diet. The good news is that veggies are equally as excellent as, if not better, whole grains regarding fiber content. Therefore, concentrate on including lots of vegetables in your diet to assist in maintaining your gastrointestinal tract functioning properly.

Per serving (1 zucchini boat), the following amounts are provided: 162 calories per serving, 6 g of total fat, 304 milligrams of sodium Carbohydrates in total: 11g, 5 g of sugar, 2 g of dietary fiber, 16 g of protein

Soup with Beef and Barley.

Traditionally made with soft beef that melts on your tongue and nutty barley, a good source of soluble fiber and B vitamins, essential for energy function. There is no need to serve this soup as a starter before the main dish because it will satisfy your appetite for the whole dinner.

- Extra-virgin olive oil (about 2 tablespoons)
- One 1/2 pound sirloin steak, cut into 1-inch chunks

- 3 little carrots, peeled and chopped 1 big parsnip, peeled and chopped 2 large carrots, diced 1 celery stalk, peeled and sliced

- 1 can tomato paste (about 6 ounces)

- 1 tablespoon dried thyme (optional)

- 1 teaspoon Worcestershire sauce (optional)

- 2 tablespoons of red wine vinegar (optional)

- a quarter cup of quick-cook barley

- 2 quarts of beef broth

- 2 quarts of water

- 1/4 cup fresh flat-leaf parsley, finely chopped

- Heat the olive oil in a large stockpot or Dutch oven over medium heat until shimmering. Cook the sirloin chunks for about 5 minutes, turning them over to brown them on all sides.

- The meat should be taken out of the saucepan and kept aside.

- Combine the onion, celery, carrots, and parsnip in a large saucepan. Cook until the vegetables are soft, approximately 5 minutes.

- Combine the tomato paste, thyme, Worcestershire sauce, and red wine vinegar in a large mixing bowl until well combined.

- Stir the steak and barley together in the pot until everything is completely covered.

- Combine the broth and water in a large mixing bowl.

- Simmer for 30 minutes, or until the barley is tender and the meat has been properly cooked, then turn down the heat to low.

- Serve with a sprinkling of fresh parsley on top, if desired.

Per serving (1 cup), there are the following calories: Calories in 1 serving: 289 13 g of total fat Sodium: 288 milligrams Carbohydrates in total: 23g 5 g of sugar 5 g of dietary fiber 20 g of protein

Beef and broccoli

There's no need to order Chinese takeout when you can prepare delicious beef and broccoli at home instead. Enjoy this recipe, rich with salty-sweet flavor and enough mixed veggies to provide you with those important antioxidants. That means it'll be even better for lunch the next day because it reheats wonderfully.

- a quarter cup of beef broth

- 3 tbsp. apple cider vinegar (optional)

- 3 tablespoons low-sodium soy sauce or Bragg Liquid Aminos (or a combination thereof)

- 2 tablespoons brown sugar (optional)

- 1/4 teaspoon red pepper flakes 1 tablespoon cornstarch 2 teaspoons minced ginger 1 tablespoon water

- 1 teaspoon sesame oil (optional)

- minced garlic (about 2 tablespoons)

- 34-inch pieces of flank steak (1 pound flank steak)

- 1 cup broccoli florets (cut into pieces)

- 1 red bell pepper, peeled and sliced into thin strips

- 2 stalks of bokchoy, thinly sliced

- Drain 1 can (8 ounces) of water chestnuts and set aside.

- Using a small mixing bowl, combine the broth, apple cider vinegar, soy sauce, brown sugar, cornstarch, ginger, and red pepper flakes until well combined. Stir until the sugar is completely dissolved. Make a mental note to put it away.

- Heat the sesame oil in a large pan over medium heat until shimmering. Add the garlic and cook for approximately 30 seconds or until it is fragrant. Cook the steak for 2 to 3 minutes per side, depending on how thick it is. Toss the meat in a large mixing dish and set aside.

- While the pan is still on medium heat, add the broccoli and red bell pepper and cook for 2 to 3 minutes, turning regularly, until the broccoli is crisp-tender.

- 3 to 5 minutes later, add the bokchoy and water chestnuts, and continue to stir until the bokchoy begins to wilt.

- Toss the steak and sauce into the skillet and cook until the beef is no longer pink. Cook, frequently stirring, for 7 to 10 minutes longer or until the sauce thickens, the veggies are soft, and the beef is cooked through (no longer pink inside), depending on how thick you want your sauce.

- As a result of the high density of the flesh and the difficulty in mechanically digesting it, beef is not always well accepted following surgery.

However, you may substitute chicken or shrimp for the beef in this recipe and still have a wonderful, protein-rich lunch.

Per serving (1 cup), there are the following calories: Calories in one serving: 187 5 g of total fat 461 milligrams of sodium Carbohydrates in total: 13g 5 g of sugar 2 g of dietary fiber 19 g of protein

Slow-Cooked Philly Cheesesteak Sandwiches.

This dish for slow-cooked beef with traditional Philly cheesesteak toppings but with a healthy twist is a must-try. The slow-cooked beef is soft and tasty, and it is an excellent choice if you are just beginning to experiment with eating more red meat regularly. While doughy bread items are not well accepted following weight-loss surgery and should be avoided to help keep carbohydrate counts down, most individuals discover that they can handle them eventually—but the thinner the bread, the better—after a few weeks (no large deli rolls).

1/20 pounds of boneless beef chuck roast

- fresh ground black pepper (about 1/2 teaspoon)

- 1/2 teaspoon fresh or dried marjoram

- Extra-virgin olive oil (about 2 tablespoons)

- 1 big onion, peeled and sliced

- 1 red bell pepper, peeled and sliced into thin strips

- 1 yellow bell pepper, thinly sliced (or sliced into strips)

- 8 ounces (2 1/2 cups) approx. tiny portabella mushrooms, thinly sliced

- 1/2 cup dry red cooking wine (optional)

- one-and-a-half tablespoons Worcestershire sauce

- 1/2 cup tomato sauce from a can

- 6 sprouted-grain hot dog buns (such as Angelic Bakehouse's) or sandwich thins (such as Angelic Bakehouse)

- Provolone cheese (around 1/2 cup shredded)

- Season the meat with pepper and marjoram before serving.

- Heat the olive oil in a large pan over medium heat until shimmering. Sear the beef on both sides for about 3 minutes per side, depending on how thick it is. Transfer the steak to a slow cooker and set the timer for 6 hours.

- Stir in the red and yellow bell peppers and simmer for another 2 to 3 minutes or until the peppers begin to soften. Remove from the heat and set aside. Cook for another 1 minute after adding the mushrooms.

- Bring the cooking wine and Worcestershire sauce to a boil in a separate saucepan. Turn off the heat and remove the skillet from the stove.

- Pour the veggies and sauce mixture over the roast and toss to coat the meat. Cook meat on low for 7 hours, turning once, until it's soft and cooked, covered in a slow cooker.

- Remove the roast from the slow cooker and carefully transfer it to a chopping board to cool. Thinly slice the roast beef to serve.

- Combine the tomato sauce and water in the slow cooker until everything is thoroughly blended.

- Toast the buns until they are golden brown.

- Half of each bun should be filled with meat, and the other half should be filled with the veggies in the tomato sauce. Top each with a slice of provolone cheese and the other half of the bread, then cut into slices and serve.

Per serving (1 sandwich), the following amounts are provided: Calories in a serving: 306 10 g of total fat Sodium: 386 milligrams Carbohydrates in total: 24g 2 g of sugar 1 gram of fiber 30 g of protein

Mom's Sloppy Joes- a family favorite.

Prepared with nutritious ingredients, more tastes, and less salt than the prepackaged canned counterparts, this American staple will transport you back to your youth.

- Cooking spray with a nonstick coating
- Ground beef that is 1 1/2 pounds of super lean beef
- 1 cup finely minced onion
- 1-1/2 cups finely chopped celery (8-ounce can of tomato sauce)

- 1/3 cup catsup (without high-fructose corn syrup)

- 2 tablespoons white vinegar (optional)

- Worcestershire sauce (about 2 teaspoons)

- mustard dijon (about 2 teaspoons)

- 1 tablespoon brown sugar (optional)

- 8 Thin sandwich rolls made entirely of whole grains, such as Thomas' sandwich thins (optional)

- Apply cooking spray in a big pan and heat it over medium heat until it is hot but not smoking. Cook the beef for about 10 minutes until it is no longer pink in the center. Any grease should be drained.

- Cook for 2 to 3 minutes, often stirring, after which add the onion and celery.

- Mix in the tomato sauce, catsup, vinegar, Worcestershire sauce, mustard, and brown sugar until everything is well-combined. Simmer the liquid for about 10 minutes, then turn the heat low. Allow 15 minutes for the sauce to thicken or until desired consistency is reached.

- When ready to serve, toast the sandwich buns (if using), then spoon about 34 cups of sloppy joe onto each roll or dish.

- Because this dish has so much flavor, it may be eaten without the bun, which helps to keep the carbohydrate count down. Otherwise, start with these sloppy joes, served open-faced on half of a narrow toasted bun and topped with cheese.

Per serving (about 34 cups): Calories in a serving: 269 5 g of total fat Sodium (mg): 656mg Total carbohydrates (g): 32g 6 g of sugar 6 g of dietary fiber 24 g of protein

Low-Carb Cheeseburger Casserole.

There used to be nothing quite like a cheeseburger and fries to satiate you after a long day at work and to fill the hole in an empty stomach—at least, that was the case. It doesn't follow that you can't eat greasy or fried foods after weight-loss surgery; you may still enjoy something that is just as cheesy and meaty yet contains potatoes.

- Cravings are kept under control.

- Cooking spray with a nonstick coating

- 2 lbs. of super lean hamburger ground beef

- 1 medium-sized onion, minced

- minced garlic (about 2 tablespoons)

- 8 tiny red potatoes, peeled and rinsed, with any defects removed and sliced into 1 1/4-inch slice

- 2 quail eggs

- 1 can tomato paste (about 6 ounces)

- 1 cup skim milk (or nonfat milk)

- 1/4 teaspoon freshly ground black pepper, freshly ground

- cheese (about 2 cups shredded Cheddar)

- Preheat the oven to 350 degrees Fahrenheit.

- Apply cooking spray in a big pan and heat it over medium heat until it is hot but not smoking. Season with salt and pepper and cook for approximately 10 minutes until the ground beef is no longer pink and the onion is soft. Remove the extra fat from the pan and set it aside.

• Spray a 9-by-13-inch casserole dish with nonstick cooking spray and set aside. Potato slices should be arranged in a layer on the bottom of the plate.

• Whisk together the eggs, tomato paste, milk, and pepper in a medium-sized mixing bowl until thoroughly incorporated, about 2 to 3 minutes.

• To assemble, layer the meat and onion on top of the potatoes, followed by the egg mixture. Next, sprinkle the Cheddar cheese over the top of the dish in a uniform layer. Aluminum foil should be used to cover the dish.

- Preheat the oven to 350°F. Remove the foil and bake for another 10 minutes, or until the potatoes are soft and the cheese begins to brown. Remove from the oven and serve immediately.

3 1/4 cups (per serving) Calories: 244 calories per serving 1/2 g of total fat 207 milligrams of sodium Carbohydrates in total: 11g 3 g of sugar 1 gram of fiber 23 g of protein

Asian Pork Tenderloin in the Slow Cooker.

Pork tenderloin is a lean cut of meat high in protein and saturated fat, which can block the arteries. Put this tenderloin in your slow cooker first thing in the morning, and you'll have a delicious hot supper waiting for you when you get home. To accompany this melt-in-your-mouth pork, seasoned with ginger-inspired ingredients, serve Asian Cucumber Salad (see recipe here). This is also a fantastic freezer dinner that can be prepared ahead of time. Follow the first and second procedures, place the ingredients in a zip-top bag and freeze them. Next, simply defrost the meat for 1 to 2 days in the refrigerator before preparing it, and then follow steps 4 and 5 to create a great supper.

- 13 cup light soy sauce or Bragg Liquid Aminos (or a combination thereof)

- 1/4 cup light brown sugar

- Worcestershire sauce (about 2 teaspoons)

- lemon juice (about 2 tablespoons) that has been freshly squeezed

- 2 teaspoons rice vinegar (optional).

- 1 tablespoon ground ginger 1 tablespoon dry mustard 1 tablespoon ground ginger

- 11/2 tablespoons freshly ground black pepper, freshly ground 4 garlic cloves, minced (about 4 pounds) pork tenderloin (also known as tenderloin de porc)

- Add the soy sauce, brown sugar, Worcestershire sauce, lemon juice, rice vinegar, dry mustard, ginger, pepper, and garlic in a gallon-size zip-top bag. Seal the bag and set it aside for later use.

- Place the pork in a zip-top bag and close it. Massage the marinade into the meat to coat it well.

- Refrigerate for at least 20 minutes or overnight to allow flavors to blend.

- Place the pork and marinade in a slow cooker and simmer on low for 4 to 6 hours or until the meat is tender. You may bake it for 30 to 40 minutes at 375 degrees Fahrenheit in a preheated oven until it reaches a minimum internal temperature of 1/45 degrees F.

- When the pork is finished, it will be soft and virtually fall apart in your mouth.

- Serve as soon as possible.

Per serving (4 ounces), there are the following calories: Calories: 256 per serving, 9 g of total fat Sodium: 658 milligrams Carbohydrates in total: 9g, 8 g of sugar, 0g of dietary fiber, 34 g of total protein

Pork Chops with Creamy Ranch Sauce

This traditional comfort meal dish is much better when cooked entirely from scratch with fresh ingredients. It's possible to prepare this the night before in the slow cooker, chill the crock, and then turn on the slow cooker just before you leave the house in the morning. Knowing that when you return home from work, there will be a great hot supper waiting for you helps the hours fly by even faster. Pork, which may be a tough cut of meat when cooked, becomes soft and falls apart when served with this dish. Pork chops can be eaten with vegetables to keep carbohydrate intake under control, or they can be served over potatoes.

- pork chops (either top loin or center loin slices) (8 ounces each), bone-in, with skin

- 1 dish (recipe) Homemade Cream of Mushroom Soup in a Condensed Form

- 1 cup skim milk (or nonfat milk)

- 1 cup chicken broth (optional)

- Ranch Seasoning (about 2 teaspoons)

- Place the pork chops in a slow cooker and cover them with the mushroom soup, milk, and broth. Cook on low for 8 hours or on high for 4 hours.

- Mix in the ranch seasoning until everything is fully coated.

- Cook on low for 6 hours with the lid on the slow cooker if you have one. Then, when the pork chops are soft and practically falling off the bone, they are ready to be served.

- Serve as soon as possible.

Pork (as well as all other meats, eggs, and dairy products) is a rich source of vitamin B1/2, essential for avoiding anemia and maintaining normal nerve activity in the body. In addition, many people require a vitamin B1/2 supplement as a tablet or an injection following bariatric surgery because of changes in the absorption of vitamin B1/2 and the danger of developing a deficit due to the procedure.

Per serving (1/2 pork chops): cal. per pound Calories in a serving: 180 6 g of total fat Sodium: 700 milligrams Carbohydrates in total: 1/4g 3 g of sugar 1 gram of fiber 13 g of protein

Naked Pulled Pork.

Look at this slow-cooked Texas-style pulled pork recipe, which transforms a tough piece of meat into something oh-so-soft. Toss the pork with a nutritious creamy coleslaw to balance out the fiery flavors in the pork, and enjoy!

In the case of the pork

- a can of tomato sauce (about 15 ounces)
- 3 tablespoons onion powder (optional).
- garlic powder (approximately 2 teaspoons)
- 1 tablespoon cumin seeds, ground
- 1 tablespoon brown sugar (optional)
- 2 teaspoons Chili Powder (optional)
- 1 teaspoon of cinnamon, ground
- 1/2 teaspoon cayenne pepper, freshly ground

- 2 pounds of pork shoulder that have been stripped of any extra fat

- 1 medium onion, peeled and chopped

- To make the creamy coleslaw

- 2/3 cup plain Greek yogurt (low-fat or nonfat)

- 2 tbsp apple cider vinegar (optional)

- freshly squeezed lemon juice (around 1 tablespoon)

- 1 teaspoon honey 1 teaspoon Dijon mustard 1 teaspoon tarragon

- 1 teaspoon onion powder (optional)

- 1 teaspoon celery seed (optional)

- Green cabbage (about 2 cups) shredded

- Red cabbage (about 2 cups) shredded

- 1 cup shredded carrots (optional)

- 1/2 cup scallions, finely chopped

For the pork, prepare the following:

- In a small mixing bowl, combine the tomato sauce, onion powder, garlic powder, cumin, brown sugar, chili powder, cinnamon, and cayenne pepper until well combined and well-flavored.

- Place the pork shoulder and onion in a slow cooker and pour the sauce over them. Cook on low for 8 to 10 hours.

- Cook on low for 6 hours with the lid on the slow cooker if you have one.

- The final pork should be easily shreddable. To shred the pork in the slow cooker, use two forks. If there is any residual sauce, boil the pork on low for another 20 minutes to let the meat absorb the remaining liquid.

- To make the coleslaw, use the following ingredients:

- In a small mixing bowl, combine the yogurt, vinegar, lemon juice, honey, mustard, onion powder, and celery seed until well combined.

- Toss the green and red cabbage, carrots, and scallions in a large mixing basin. Using your hands, mix the veggies in the dressing until fully coated. Refrigerate the coleslaw overnight to achieve the best results.

- Serve the pork on a bed of coleslaw to finish it off.

Per Serving (1/2 cup pork with 1/2 cup coleslaw): calories are as follows: 260 calories per serving, 11 g of total fat Sodium: 705 milligrams Carbohydrates in total: 20 g 10 g of sugar, 5 g of dietary fiber, 20 g of protein.

Chapter Six

Desserts

Fruit-Infused Waters

Even though artificial sweeteners are completely acceptable to consume after surgery, there is something to be said about attempting to drink clean liquids free of sugar and artificial sweeteners. Excessive consumption of sugary beverages may result in a desire for additional sweet meals for certain persons. Infused waters are a delicious choice for those who want a savory drink without sugar or a sugar replacement. And when it comes to deciding what to add to your fruit-infused water, the possibilities are endless—be creative and try different herbs and spices to see what works best for you. In addition, increasing the taste of your water may assist you in meeting your daily hydration requirements.

Options for infusers include:

- 3 to 5 cucumber slices, 2 lime wedges, and 4 fresh mint leaves are all you need for this dish.

- 4 sliced strawberries and 1 sliced jalapeno pepper (optional)

- 4 fresh basil leaves and 1/4 cup cubed watermelon are all you need.

- 134 cup grapefruit wedges and 1 fresh rosemary sprig (with stem removed), 2 or 3 blackberries, 1/8 cup blueberries, and 2 orange wedges are all good options.

- Lemon wedges, lime wedges, and orange wedges (a total of four)

- 2 cucumber slices, 1/2 fresh lavender sprigs, stemmed, 3 fresh mint leaves, and 2 lemon wedges are all you need to make this dish.

- 1/4 apple, sliced, and 1 teaspoon of ground cinnamon or 1 cinnamon stick are combined in this recipe.

- Combine any preceding combinations with at least 2 cups of water to form a smooth paste.

- To bring out the tastes of the herbs, muddle them in the fruit with a wooden spoon or a muddler until they are well combined.

- Consider using an infuser bottle or pitcher to help separate seeds and herbs from the drinking section of the water so that they do not mix with the drinkable portion.

Per serving (1 cup), there are the following calories: Calories in a serving: 0 0 g of total fat Sodium: 0 milligrams Carbohydrates in total: 0g 0 g of sugar 0g of dietary fiber 0 g of protein

Mint Lemonade is a refreshing drink.

Sugary beverages should be eliminated from your diet following bariatric surgery, but you should not feel forced to drink only plain water all of the time after surgery. This delightful take on lemonade will add some diversity to your beverage repertoire. It's produced using stevia, a plant-based sweetener with no calories and no carbs yet is sweeter than sugar since it comes from plants.

- 2 lemons squeezed into a glass 2 sprigs of mint, fresh from the garden

- 1/2 teaspoon stevia powder (optional) 4 quarts of water

- Ice

- Use a wooden spoon or a muddler to muddle the lemon juice, mint leaves, and stevia in a small pitcher, pressing down on the mint to release the oils.

- Fill the pitcher halfway with water and ice and set it aside.

Per serving (1 cup), there are the following calories: 5 calories per serving, 0 g of total fat Sodium: 0 milligrams Carbohydrates in total: 1 g 0 g of sugar, 0g of dietary fiber, 0 g of protein

Fudge Brownies with a healthier twist.

These brownies include a secret ingredient that no one who eats them (except you, the maker) will ever, ever guess is in them. The component in question is beans—specifically, black beans. While the beans do not affect the brownies' flavor, they contribute to creating an enticing fudgy texture. In addition to being tastier than the boxed version, they're also lower in sugar and fat than the boxed version. So bring these goodies to your next potluck, party, or birthday celebration as a treat you can enjoy without feeling guilty about eating too much sugar.

- Cooking spray with a nonstick coating

- 1 (1/4.5-ounce) can black beans, drained and rinsed 1 (1/4.5-ounce) can white beans 3 quail eggs

- 3 tbsp. extra-virgin olive oil

- 1/4 cup unsweetened cocoa powder (optional) 1 teaspoon pure vanilla extract (optional)

- 13 cups granulated sugar (optional)

- 1 teaspoon instant coffee (optional) (optional)

- 1/2 cup semi-sweet chocolate chips

- Preheat the oven to 350 degrees Fahrenheit. Spray an 8-by-8-inch square baking dish with nonstick cooking spray and set aside.

- Pour all ingredients into a blender and process until smooth and lump-free. Next, add the black beans, eggs, canola oil, cocoa powder, vanilla, sugar, and coffee (if using).

- Pour the ingredients into the baking dish and put the chocolate chips on top. Bake for 30 minutes at 350 degrees.

- Bake for about 30 minutes, or until the top is dry and the edges of the pan begin to come away from the sides of the pan.

- Cut the brownies into 16 pieces and serve.

Per serving (1 brownie), the following amounts are provided: Calories in a serving: 1/24 6 g of total fat Sodium: 18 milligrams Carbohydrates in total: 16 g 7 g of sugar 5 g of dietary fiber 4 g of protein

Pumpkin Mousse with a Creamy Texture.

Nothing says autumn quite like a pumpkin pie. This creamy, smooth texture makes it the ideal component for a delectable dessert. This mousse has a cheesecake-like texture, which will satisfy your sweet taste when you make it. Instead of conventional cream cheese, try using Neufchâtel cream cheese to save a few calories and a few grams of saturated fat. Finally, don't forget to sprinkle the cinnamon on top to complete this delectable dessert, which is so delicious that you'll want to serve it all year long.

- a box of Neufchâtel cream cheese (8 ounces) at room temperature 15-ounce can of pumpkin puree (optional)

- 2 cups skimmed or fat-free milk

- Pumpkin pie spice (about 2 tablespoons) 2 tablespoons stevia extract (liquid)

- 1 teaspoon pure vanilla extract (optional)

- 1 teaspoon of cinnamon, ground

- Using a hand mixer, whip together the cream cheese and pumpkin puree in a medium-sized mixing bowl until smooth and thoroughly mixed.

- After adding the milk, pumpkin pie spice, stevia, and vanilla continue to blend for another 5 minutes or until the mixture is light and airy in consistency.

- Divide the mousse evenly among the serving glasses, then sprinkle the cinnamon on top of each serving glass. Refrigerate until you're ready to use it (around 30 minutes).

- Pumpkin is a rich source of beta-carotene, an antioxidant found to fight cancer-causing free radicals in the body and protect against heart disease and other chronic diseases. Carrots and squash are two more foods that are high in beta-carotene.

Per serving (around 2 1/3 cups): Calories in a serving: 151 10 g of total fat Sodium: 177 milligrams Carbohydrates in total: 7g 0g of dietary fiber 5 g of sugar 6 g of protein

Parfaits with vanilla cheesecake.

- Inhale the sweet and tangy flavors of a newly picked strawberry, blueberry, or blackberry at the peak of their season, and you will feel an explosion of sweet and tart flavors on your tongue. These berries are the ideal complement to a rich and creamy cheesecake filling, as shown in the photo. Tofu is a secret ingredient in this recipe to give it a creamy texture without adding more fat or calories to the dish. When it comes to serving, be sure to use crystal-clear glasses.

- a quarter-cup of plain Greek yogurt (low-fat)

- 3 ounces silken tofu (optional) (about one-fifth of a 16-ounce package)

- sugar cane extract powdered 1/4 teaspoon stevia extract vanilla extract (about 2 tablespoons)

- 1 cup blackberries, quartered or quartered again

- 1 cup strawberries, quartered after they have been stemmed 1 cup berries (blueberries)

- 4 sprigs of fresh mint

- A hand mixer on medium-high speed may be used to combine the yogurt, tofu, stevia, and vanilla extract in a large mixing bowl until the mixture is creamy, frothy, and fully smooth.

- Prepare 4 small (8-ounce) glasses to layer the parfaits before assembling them.

- The parfaits are assembled by layering blackberries at their base, a spoonful of the yogurt mixture on top of the blackberries, a layer of strawberries, and a final dollop of the yogurt mixture on top of that. Next, layer the blueberries on top of the yogurt mixture, then finish with a final dollop of the yogurt mixture. Finally, each glass should be garnished with a mint leaf.

- Refrigerate until you're ready to use it (around 30 minutes).

- Berries are a wonderful source of vitamins and antioxidants and are considered a top superfood that should be included in one's daily diet. A distinct hue denotes a different phytochemical that has been shown to have favorable effects on the body. Change up the berries in this recipe to include your favorite fresh berries, such as raspberries (red or white), black currants, tart cranberries, or whatever is in season and accessible to you.

1 parfait contains the following calories: Calories in a serving: 103 2 g of total fat Sodium: 28 milligrams Carbohydrates in total: 15 g 9 g of sugar 4 g of dietary fiber 6 g of protein

Lemon Bars.

A tangy, sour lemon dessert is a lovely and refreshing treat after a long day. With these lemon bars, you won't have to worry about going overboard with your sugar consumption because they're low in sugar. They are produced using stevia extract, which helps to limit the number of calories and carbs to a bare minimum. While coconut oil should be used in moderation since it contains saturated fat, it is a good substitute for butter and lard when used in small amounts. In this case, it makes it feasible to have a crispy crust.

To make the crust

- Cooking spray with a nonstick coating

- 1/4 cups stevia baking mix 1 cup whole-wheat pastry flour 1 cup oat bran

- 1/4 cup coconut oil (optional)

- To make the lemon filling

- 4 quail eggs

- 2 egg yolks (optional)

- 1/2 cup stevia baking blend (optional) 4 lemons squeezed into a glass

- 2 tbsp. coconut oil (optional)

- For the crust, use the following ingredients:

- Preheat the oven to 350 degrees Fahrenheit. Spray a 9-by-13-inch baking pan with nonstick cooking spray and set aside.

- To make the mixture coarse, place the flour, stevia, and coconut oil in a medium mixing bowl and blend with a hand mixer on medium-high speed until well combined.

- Spread a thin mixture layer onto the bottom of a baking pan, pushing it into the pan to create an equal layer.

- Place the pie in the oven for 20 minutes or until the crust becomes golden brown. Remove the pan from the oven, but do not turn off the oven until you have finished. Allow for around 5 minutes of cooling time before adding the filling to the crust.

- For the lemon filling, combine the following ingredients:

- The eggs, egg yolks, and stevia should be whisked together until well blended in a small saucepan while the crust is baking. Next, place the pan over medium heat and add the lemon juice and coconut oil, stirring constantly. Cook the filling for 5 minutes, stirring often, or until the mixture thickens a little bit more.

- The filling should be poured over the prepared crust and baked for 1/4 to 15 minutes afterward. When the edges begin to brown, and the filling has firmed, it is time to remove it from the oven.

- Allow it to cool fully before cutting it into 24 bars and serving.

Per serving (1 bar), the following costs are incurred: Calories in one serving: 55 4 g of total fat Sodium: 13 milligrams Carbohydrates in total: 4 g 7 g of sugar 1 gram of fiber 2 g of protein

Fruit Dip with a Creamy Chocolate Flavour.

We are all aware that we should consume enough fruits and veggies throughout the day, but it can be tedious to just eat them as is. Try this fruit dip to spice up basic fruit, encouraging you to eat more. As a bonus, you will also receive a dietary source of protein.

- 1/2 cups plain Greek yogurt with no added sugar

- 1/2 cup creamy natural peanut butter, unsweetened honey (about 2 teaspoons)

- 2 tablespoons cocoa powder (unsweetened is best) 1 teaspoon pure vanilla extract (optional)

- To make the pudding, place all the ingredients in a medium mixing bowl and use a hand mixer on low speed to blend everything together until smooth and thoroughly blended.

- Refrigerate overnight or at least 30 minutes before serving to allow the flavors to melt together better.

- Keep the dish cold until you're ready to serve it.

- To complete the meal, serve with fresh fruit, such as apple, pear, or banana slices. Some patients may accept fresh fruit better post-operatively if the peel is removed, particularly while they are adjusting to eating fresh fruits and vegetables for the first time.

Per serving (1/4 cup): calories: 230 Calories in one serving: 1/20 7 g of total fat Sodium: 53 milligrams Carbohydrates in total: 10 g 1 gram of fiber 7 g of sugar 6 g of protein

Cookies with peanut butter and chocolate chips.

Chocolate chip cookies are a familiar part of our lives and cultures—whether as a snack after school dipped in milk, upon check-in at a hotel while on vacation, or at Grandma's house when you see her—and are popular with children and adults alike. So it's difficult to picture life without this delectable treat. With creamy peanut butter and heart-healthy oil, this healthier version of chocolate chip cookies is sure to please.

- 1/2 cup creamy natural peanut butter, unsweetened

- 13 cup canola oil (optional)

- a quarter cup of granulated sugar

- 1/4 cup brown sugar that has been packed 1 teaspoon pure vanilla extract (optional) 2 big eggs (about)

- 11/4 cups old-fashioned rolled oats (or equivalent) 1 cup whole-wheat pastry flour (or equivalent)

- 2 tablespoons toasted flaxseed (ground) 1 teaspoon baking soda (optional)

- dark chocolate chips (about a third of a cup) (60 percent cacao or higher)

- Preheat the oven to 350 degrees Fahrenheit.

- A hand mixer fitted with a paddle attachment may be used to cream the peanut butter, canola oil, granulated and brown sugars, and vanilla extract until they are creamy and smooth.

- Add the eggs one at a time, beating well after each addition.

- In a small mixing bowl, whisk the oats, flour, flaxseed, and baking soda until well combined.

- Using a mixer on low speed, gradually incorporate the dry ingredients into the peanut butter mixture.

- Add in the chocolate chips and mix well.

- Drop tablespoons of dough onto a baking sheet that has not been oiled, spacing them approximately 2 inches apart.

- Preparation time: approximately 9 minutes, or until the edges begin to brown.

- Wait about 1 minute before transferring the cookies to a cooling rack to finish cooling them completely before serving them.

- Flaxseed is a high-fiber, omega-3 fatty acid and alpha-linolenic acid source that is also high in protein (ALA). It has been demonstrated that flaxseed can help decrease blood pressure, among many other health advantages. To sneak it into your diet, mix a spoonful of it into your protein shake, spaghetti sauce, meatloaf, or other baked products.

Per serving (2 cookies), the following costs are incurred: 164 calories per serving, 10 g of total fat Sodium: 75 milligrams Carbohydrates in total: 17g 8 g of sugar 2 g of dietary fiber 3 g of protein

Low-Carb Chocolate Mousse.

This silky, decadent chocolate mousse will take you to another world. Because this recipe simply calls for stevia powder to sweeten it, you can enjoy dessert without worrying about the extra sugar. Instead, the chia seeds are used to make the mixture thicken organically without the use of typical components such as heavy whipped cream, such as heavy cream or yogurt. Fresh raspberries are sprinkled on top of the final mousse to give it a vibrant color and a tart finish.

- 1 cup ricotta cheese (preferably low-fat) 1 cup skim milk (or nonfat milk)

- 1 tablespoon cocoa powder (unsweetened is best) 1 tbsp. chia seeds (optional)

- 2 tablespoons of stevia extract

- 1/2 teaspoons of pure vanilla essence 1 cup of fresh raspberries

- Blend the ricotta, milk, cocoa powder, chia seeds, stevia, and vanilla on medium speed until everything is fully combined and extremely creamy.

- Distribute the mousse among four small serving glasses in an equal layers.

- Refrigerate for at least 2 hours, preferably overnight for the best results, to thicken the sauce.

- Serve by sprinkling 1/4 cup of fresh raspberries on top of each glass.

- Chia seeds are a fantastic source of fiber and omega-3 fatty acids. An incredible 4.5 grams of fiber are included in only one spoonful! Add these to your yogurt in the morning to get some extra nutrients and to help you fulfill your daily fiber goals. They're delicious!

Per 1/2-cup serving (approximately): Calories in this recipe: 113 3 g of total fat Sodium: 102 milligrams Carbohydrates in total: 13g 8 g of sugar 7 g of dietary fiber 9 g of protein

Frozen Yogurt with Raspberry Flavor.

Many patients who have had weight-loss surgery miss the taste of ice cream and frozen yogurt. But, on a hot summer day, there's nothing better than something refreshing and fruity. Fortunately, this frozen yogurt is both sweet and tangy and will fulfill your ice cream cravings without being too sugary. In addition, because it only requires four ingredients and can be prepared in less than 10 minutes, you may enjoy this dessert during summer.

- 4 cups frozen raspberries (optional)

- 1/2 cup plain Greek yogurt with no added sugar

- lemon juice (about 2 tablespoons) that has been freshly squeezed 2 tablespoons of stevia extract (liquid)

- To make the raspberry yogurt, place all ingredients in a blender or food processor and mix until smooth (approximately 5 minutes).

- Serve immediately, or store in an airtight container and use within 3 weeks after freezing.

- To keep things interesting in this frozen yogurt dish, you may substitute any of your favorite fruits. For example, try frozen strawberries, peaches, or mangoes for a refreshing treat!

Per serving (1 cup), there are the following calories: Calories in one serving: 11/4 2 g of total fat Sodium: 18 milligrams Carbohydrates in total: 19g 7 g of sugar 9 g of dietary fiber 5 g of protein.

Conclusion

There's a good chance that your connection with food started shifting when you thought about getting bariatric surgery. During the time that you are recovering after surgery and in the years to follow, you will most likely experience ongoing changes in how you think about and feel about eating.

Likely, you've already started making substantial dietary changes to be evaluated for surgery. If so, congratulations! It's possible that making even more adjustments may lessen the pleasure you get from your meals or that the concept of having to prepare food with various textures will be overwhelming. In addition, you may be worried that you won't be able to follow the directions for each post-operative stage if you are not used to doing things like cooking. This is understandable.

Bear in mind that, in the vast majority of instances, you will have your healthcare team available to you at every step of the route to provide support and guidance. In addition, the book has provided you with the essential building blocks necessary for you to succeed in the future. It is not going to be easy, and it will not happen quickly, but it will be a learning experience that will enable you to move in the direction of improved health.

BARIATRIC MEAL PREP

The ultimate bariatric meal prep full of tasty recipes and meal prep for your daily routine

CASEY CALDWELL

Introduction

There is only one answer to the problem of losing weight, and that is to actively work toward the objective. The only course of action available is to take real action. The problem can have developed as a result of poor eating habits or been passed down through the generations. Maintaining a healthy weight improves our wellbeing overall and makes it simpler for us to live pain-free. Our level of tension and anxiety decreases as a result of this. A significant quantity of body fat is removed, which lowers the risk of developing diseases like high blood pressure, osteoarthritis, sleep apnea, type 2 diabetes, renal disease, and liver disease that are linked to obesity. This is because obesity has been linked to every single one of these diseases.

When we decide to act, we could discover that there are some tough choices to make before we can start the preliminary measures necessary to improve our health. Therefore, we must make a lot of choices before we start the first steps necessary to enhance our health.

As part of the bariatric surgery procedure, the patient's stomach size may be lowered. This is one technique provided by bariatric surgery for quickly reducing excess body fat. Our stomachs will consequently be significantly smaller, which will naturally cause us to eat considerably less when we do. We will therefore experience "fullness" much more quickly as a result. As a result, when we do, we will eat far less. However, because our stomachs have drastically decreased, we will experience "fullness" much more gradually. Our stomachs would be significantly smaller as a result. We won't feel constantly hungry as a result of the therapy, and we won't feel the urge to eat unnecessarily. These two items are both lost forever. Having this choice rather than having to provide for ourselves can save us time and effort.

There are several other surgical procedures that can be used, including as gastric banding, gastric sleeve surgery, and gastric bypass surgery. However, whether or not surgery is done, the outcome will surely be a rapid and significant weight loss in the following 18 to 24 months, depending on the individual. The surgery will undoubtedly lead to this weight loss. The experts' findings suggest that most people should expect a 50% decrease in their excess body weight over this time.

Your primary care doctor or a dietitian could suggest that you start with a diet that is mostly liquid and gradually switch to one that contains less solid foods consumed at meals. A liquid-first diet is this kind of eating regimen. You need to commit to following this diet religiously if you want the best results. You should be able to return to a diet of only solid meals with no restrictions after four months. In this case, a move should be made as soon as is practical.

Given the situation, maintaining and further establishing a strategy that prioritizes healthy eating will demand the most effort from you. The air fryer is one of the most well-liked and frequently used pieces of kitchen equipment in the modern era. Because it's quick and simple to prepare lighter meals, it's a perfect alternative for anyone who wants to eat more healthfully without giving up the fun or convenience of their cuisine.

Because it gathers all of the necessary recipes in one convenient location, this cookbook makes it simple for you to prepare great meals with your Air Fryer.

Chapter One

What You Must Understand

An objective of a bariatric diet is to promote weight loss and stomach rebuilding. A bariatric diet aims to change eating patterns in order to accomplish these two objectives. Maintaining the diet will also help you avoid any unpleasant side effects or challenging challenges, which will make losing weight easier.

How to Stay Focused While Adhering to the Bariatric Diet Plan

In order to provide your body the support it needs as it gradually transitions from eating liquids to solids following surgery, a bariatric diet is frequently divided into numerous stages or phases.

Our goal with this gradual change is to give your body the best opportunity to heal. The majority of patients can return to their previous diets three months after their procedures. However, how quickly this happens will depend on how rapidly their bodies heal from the therapy and acclimate to their new eating patterns.

Which foods are best to eat and which should be avoided?

You might receive instructions to restrict your diet to only clear liquids after therapy. You can advance to drinking a range of liquids after your body gets used to drinking clear liquids, such as broth, milk, juice without added sugar, decaffeinated coffee and tea, among many more choices. You can gradually wean yourself off clear beverages thanks to this. You can move on to the next stage, which entails taking four to six tablespoons of pureed food with each meal, after letting your body about a week to get acclimated to drinking liquids. When your body has had time to acclimate to drinking liquids, you will do this. Three to six smaller meals can be had during the day. Your objective is to reduce your daily intake of soft foods from 13 cups to 1/2 cup throughout the course of the following week. Up to five meals a day may be consumed, and they may include foods that are simple to chew, such as rice, eggs, cooked fruits, and vegetables.

You can progressively start consuming foods that are more difficult for you to eat after eight weeks. Additionally, you can continue to have three meals a day. Which meals you can endure and how much of each meal you can eat will determine the variety of foods you can eat, the amount of those foods you can take, and their consistency. You should consume one nutritious meal per day that maintains your calorie intake under 1,000. Avoid fried foods, fizzy beverages, bread, raw vegetables, red meat, and meals that are heavily spiced, nut- and seed-seasoned since they can make you sick or make you feel nauseous. Dumping syndrome can be prevented by staying away from foods high in fat and sugar, which digest food more quickly than other nutrients. One strategy to guard against dumping syndrome is to avoid meals that are high in sugar.

starting with a few guidelines and pointers for getting going

Start off easy before putting more of a challenge on yourself. For instance, you should gradually introduce one new dish into your diet. Then you should progressively increase the total amount of servings you consume. Additionally, make sure you thoroughly chew your food.

Always keep an eye on your level of hydration. For example, once you've ended the phase of consuming just clear liquids, you should focus on consuming meals that are high in protein but low in fat. Additionally, you ought to make an effort to consume fewer calories each day.

Before continuing with the next phase of your bariatric eating plan, you must stay in close communication with the surgical team who performed your bariatric treatment.

Do not minimize the importance of adhering to your doctor's recommendations and taking the suggested multivitamins. After the procedure, your body won't be able to properly absorb the nutrients from the food it eats, and this condition could last the remainder of your life.

What does it mean when something is stated to be "fried" in the air?

An air fryer can produce food with the same amount of crispiness as a deep fryer with just a little hot air and oil. This can be finished without the need for any more elements. As a result, no additional parts are needed. When one considers that it is capable of baking, roasting, and grilling in addition to those other two cooking ways, it is evident that this is a versatile gadget that can be obtained for a price that is not excessively expensive.

How precisely does the procedure work?

Countertop convection ovens and air fryers both have the same functions, however the air fryer uses less energy and cooks food faster. This kitchen appliance features a heating element and a fan, allowing hot air to move fast throughout the appliance. The outcome is that the meal cooks with the maximum amount of crispiness. The Maillard reaction, a chemical process that also contributes to the food's characteristic flavor and aroma, causes food to turn brown after cooking. Hot air is used in air fryers to create the Maillard reaction, also known as the results of deep-frying food. As a result of this chemical reaction, food turns brown. Since it has parts and attachments that can be cleaned in the dishwasher, you can enjoy the flavor of deep-fried food without the mess and oil that come with traditional deep-frying techniques.

Air frying Is Associated with a Wide Range of Benefits

Dishes that could previously only be prepared in a deep frying now have a healthy alternative thanks to the air fryer. This has the effect of reducing the amount of fat in foods that are prepared in other methods, such as baking or roasting, as opposed to those that are deep-fried in hot oil.

For instance, a serving of frozen French fries cooked in an air fryer has 4 to 6 grams of fat. There are 17 grams of fat in the deep-fried version. In comparison to a deep-fried chicken breast, which has 13.2 grams of fat per 100 grams, an air-fried chicken breast has 0.39 grams of fat per 100 grams.

Utilizing an air fryer could help you lower the percentage of calories in your diet that come from fat as they use either very little or no oil. This is because air fryers use little to no oil, if any at all. Even though fat is beneficial for you, consuming too much of it can be harmful to your health. Cardiovascular disease and inflammation are two examples. These two scenarios are harmful to your health.

principles and techniques for cooking

Give your air fryer enough time to reach the right temperature. You only need to turn on the air fryer, set the temperature to your preferences, and then set the timer for two or three minutes to complete this task.

Despite any inclination you may have, you should avoid making a lot of food all at once. When an air fryer's basket is fully loaded with food, the frying of the various meals in the basket is frequently unexpected. It will also prevent food from drying out and becoming rotten. The amount of time needed to cook the meal could be considerably greater.

To successfully bake bread, it's essential to carefully adhere to the directions. It is imperative to note that many air fryer recipes call for breading and that, on occasion, the air fryer's fan may blow the breading off the food while it cooks. This needs to be stressed repeatedly. It's vital to top foods with three different ingredients: flour, eggs, and breadcrumbs. Give the breadcrumbs some time to settle and work very hard to distribute them evenly around the plate.

It is best to use toothpicks to secure food while using an air fryer because the fan has the power to stir up tiny, light food particles.

There is an alternative to the typical application techniques of drizzling or brushing: spraying oil from a bottle onto a plate. Spraying oil over the food is easier and consumes the least amount of oil throughout the entire meal. One advantage of cooking with oil is this. It's likely that some commercial oil sprays contain substances that could damage the air fryer basket's nonstick coating. Keep as far away from this as you can. It is a good idea to purchase a spray bottle for the kitchen that must be manually activated because these chemicals have the potential to be dangerous.

To help the food brown and crisp up more thoroughly than it would on its own, spritz the dish with oil spray halfway through cooking. This is because the oil spray contains a lot of polyunsaturated fatty acids. Additionally, because they cook at the same time every time, alternating the meals will produce food that is prepared more consistently.

If the basket is thoroughly shaken at regular intervals, the various flavors and ingredients will be distributed equally throughout the meal preparation. Additionally, this will produce dishes that crisp and brown more consistently throughout the cooking process.

While cooking food in the air fryer basket, you can prevent undesired smoke from coming out of the device because the oil has reached an intolerably high temperature by adding water to the drawer underneath the basket.

You are welcome to open the air fryer whenever you feel the need to do so and check on the status of the meal. Knowing that this won't impede the cooking process allows you to relax. In this circumstance, there is absolutely no reason to be afraid.

Chapter Two

Breakfast

Broccoli Muffins

Preparation time: 24 minutes

Ingredients:

- 2 big eggs cup broccoli florets, finely chopped (serves 6 people)

- cups unsweetened almond milk 1 cup almond flour 1 tsp baking powder 1 cup almond milk

- 2 Tbsps. Yeast extract (nutritional yeast) is used to supplement the diet with essential nutrients such as protein, iron, and zinc.

- 1/2 teaspoons sea salt

Directions:

- Preheat the air fryer to 325 degrees Fahrenheit.

- Combine all ingredients in a large mixing basin until everything is well-combined.

- Fill the silicone muffin molds halfway with the batter and set them in the air fryer basket.

- Cook muffins for 20 to 24 minutes at 375°F.

- Prepare the dish and serve it.

Nutrition:

- 260 calories per serving

- 21.2 g of total fat

- 11 g of carbohydrate calories

- 1.7 g of sugar

- 1/2 g of protein

- Cholesterol: 62 milligrams

Gratin de Zucchini (Zucchini Gratin).

Preparation time: 24 minutes 4 portions (servings)

Ingredients:

- 1 big egg, gently beaten 1 large egg, lightly beaten

- If desired, unsweetened almond milk (1/4 cup), 3 medium zucchinis, cut 1 tablespoon of olive oil.

- 1/2 cup nutritional yeast (optional) 1 teaspoon of sea salt

Directions:

- Preheat the air fryer to 370 degrees Fahrenheit.

- Prepare a baking dish for the air fryer by arranging zucchini slices.

- Stir in the Dijon mustard, nutritional yeast, and sea salt to the almond milk in a saucepan over low heat until it is warm. Whisk in the beaten egg until it is well incorporated.

- Cook the meal in the air fryer for 20-24 minutes, depending on the size of the dish.

- Prepare the dish and serve it.

Nutrition:

- Calories in one serving: 1/20

- 3.4 g of fat

- There are 1/4 grams of carbohydrates in this recipe.

- 2 g of sugar

- 13 g of protein

- Cholesterol: 47 milligrams

Egg Bites with Pepper.

Preparation time: 15 minutes Number of servings: 7

Ingredients:

- 5 big eggs, beaten to a frothy 3 tablespoons milk with a 2 percent fat content

- 1/2 tsp. Marjoram, 1 tsp. Salt-dried tsp.

- peppercorns that have been freshly ground

- 13 cups finely chopped bell pepper (of any color) 3 tablespoons finely minced scallions

- 1/2 cup shredded Colby or Muenster cheese, to taste

Directions:

- Stir until well blended in a medium-sized mixing basin. Add marjoram and season to taste with salt and black pepper.

- Combine the bell peppers, scallions, and cheese in a large mixing bowl. Fill each of the 7 egg bite cups halfway with the egg mixture, being careful you get some of the solids in each cup. Set the egg bite cups aside. Preheat the air fryer to 325 degrees Fahrenheit or set it to that temperature.

- Make a foil sling by following these steps: Fold an 18-inch-long sheet of heavy-duty aluminum foil in thirds lengthwise to create a triangular shape. Using this sling, lift the egg bite pan into the air fryer and drop it into the oven.

- The foil should be left in the air fryer, but it should be bent down to fit in the device.

- 10 to 15 minutes, or until a toothpick inserted into the middle comes out clean, is required for baking the egg bits.

- Remove the egg bite pan from the oven with the help of the foil sling. Allow for 5 minutes of cooling time before inverting the pan onto a dish to remove the egg bits. Warm the dish before serving.

Nutrition:

- Calories in a serving: 87

- 6 g of total fat 3 g of saturated fat Cholesterol: 1/41 milligrams Sodium: 1/49 milligrams 1 gram of carbohydrates Fiber:0g

- 7 g of protein

Crunchy Nut Granola.

Time required for preparation: 10 minutes Preparation time: 15 minutes 6 individual servings

Ingredients:

- 2 cups old-fashioned oats, rolled 1/4 cup pistachios 1/4 cup pecans, chopped 1/4 cup cashews, chopped 1/4 cup honey 2 cups old-fashioned oats, rolled

- 2 tbsp. Light brown sugar, to taste, 3 tbsp. extra-virgin olive oil

- 1/2 tsp. freshly ground cinnamon

- Baking spray with a nonstick coating (containing flour)

- 1/2 cup dried cherries (optional)

Directions:

- Toss the oats, pistachios, pecans, and cashews in a medium-sized mixing bowl until well combined.

- Heat the honey, brown sugar, vegetable oil, and cinnamon in a small saucepan until the sugar is dissolved. Cook over low heat, stirring regularly, for 4 minutes or until the mixture is smooth and completely smooth. Pour the liquid over the oat mixture and stir well.

- A 7-inch springform pan should be sprayed with baking spray. Add the granola mixture to the bowl.

- Preheat the air fryer to 325 degrees Fahrenheit or set it to that temperature. Place the pan in the air fryer basket and close the lid. Cook for 7 minutes before removing the pan from the heat and stirring. Continue to heat for another 6 to 9 minutes or until the granola is a light golden brown, stirring occasionally. Add in the dried cherries and mix well.

- Remove the pan from the air fryer and set it aside to cool, stirring the granola a couple of times as it cools. Store at room temperature for up to 4 days in a tightly sealed container.

Nutrition:

- Calories in a serving: 446 18 g of total fat 5 g of Saturated Fatty Acids 15 milligrams of cholesterol Sodium: 51 milligrams

- 64 g of carbohydrates

- Fiber:7g 11 g of protein

Frittata with vegetables.

Time required for preparation: 25 minutes 4 portions (servings)

The recipe contains the following ingredients:

1/4 cup red bell pepper, chopped; 1/4 cup yellow summer squash, chopped; 2 tbsp. scallion, chopped; 5 big eggs, beaten; 1/4 teaspoon sea salt; 2 teaspoons freshly ground black pepper; 1 cup Cheddar cheese, shredded and split.

Directions:

- Combine the bell pepper, summer squash, and scallion in a 7-inch cake pan and bake for 30 minutes.

- Preheat the air fryer to 350 degrees Fahrenheit, if necessary. Place the cake pan in the air fryer basket and close the lid. Cook the veggies for 3 to 4 minutes or until they are crisp-tender, depending on how large they are. Remove the pan from the air fryer and set it aside.

- Whisk together the eggs, salt, and pepper in a medium-sized mixing bowl. Add half of the Cheddar and mix well. Pour the sauce into the pan with the veggies.

- Return the pan to the air fryer and cook for another 10 to 15 minutes before sprinkling the remaining cheese on top and serving. Cook for 4 to 5 minutes or until the cheese is melted and the frittata is set, whichever comes first. To serve, cut the fruit into wedges.

Nutrition:

- 260 calories total fat: 21 grams saturated fat: 11 grams Cholesterol: 277 milligrams 463 milligrams of sodium 2 g of carbohydrates

- Fiber:0g 15 g of protein

Potatoes for breakfast.

Preparation time: 23 minutes 4 portions (servings)

Ingredients:

- 8 medium russet potatoes, cleaned and diced, 1/2 teaspoon sea-salt

- 1 tablespoon extra-virgin olive oil

- 1/4 tsp. Garlic powder (optional) garnished with parsley, finely chopped

Directions:

- Place the potatoes in a large bowl of cold water, soak for 45 minutes, then drain and dry.

- In the Air Fryer basket, toss the potato cubes with the garlic powder, salt, and olive oil until well combined.

- Close the lid of the Air Fryer toaster oven after placing the Air Fryer basket within it. Select the Air Fry mode at 400oF for 23 minutes at that temperature.

- When they're half-cooked, toss them thoroughly and continue to cook until they're done.

To finish, garnish with chopped parsley before serving.

Nutrition:

- Calories in one serving: 1/46 6.2 g of protein Carbohydrates: 41.2 g 5 g of fat

Avocado Flautist

Preparation time: 24 minutes Ingredients: 8 servings (serves 8)

- 1 tablespoon extra-virgin olive oil 8 eggs, lightly beaten

- 1/2 teaspoons salt and 1/4 teaspoons pepper 1 1/2 teaspoon cumin

- 1 teaspoon of chili powder, 8 tortillas, fajita-size, 4 oz. softened cream cheese (optional). 8 pieces of bacon, browned

- Avocado Crème (sometimes known as "Avocado Crème"):

- 2 small avocados (about)

- 1/2 cup plain Greek yogurt 1 lime, freshly squeezed

- 1/2 teaspoon of salt

- peppercorns (1/4 tsp.)

Directions:

- In a pan, heat the olive oil over medium heat, then add the eggs, salt, cumin, pepper, and chili powder, stirring for 4 minutes. Spread cream cheese on the tortillas and then top them with bacon bits. Afterward, evenly distribute the egg scramble on top and sprinkle with cheese.

- Rolling the tortillas helps to keep the contents inside the tortillas. 4 rolls should be placed in the Air Fryer basket. Close the lid of the Air Fryer toaster oven after placing the Air Fryer basket within it. Select the Air Fry option at 400 degrees Fahrenheit for 1/2 minute at the highest temperature.

- Cook the remaining tortilla rolls in the same manner as you did the first batch. Meanwhile, combine the avocado crème in a blender and serve with the heated flautas.

Nutrition:

- Calories: 21/2 per serving 17.3 g of protein Carbohydrates: 1/4.6 g 11.8 g of fat

Frittata with ham, mushrooms, and tomatoes.

Preparation time: 16 minutes

Ingredients: Ingredients: Servings: 2

- chopped 1 cooked ham slice 1 ham slice 6 cherry tomatoes, peeled and halved

- 6 fresh mushrooms, chopped into thin slices

- Season with salt and freshly ground black pepper as needed. 3 quail eggs

- 1 tablespoon finely chopped fresh parsley

Directions:

- Mix the ham, tomatoes, mushrooms, salt, and black pepper in a baking pan until everything is evenly distributed.

- To choose the "Air Fry" mode, press the "Power Button" on the Air Fry Oven and turn the dial to the right.

- To adjust the cooking time to 16 minutes, press the Time button twice more and spin the dial one more.

- Now, press the Temp button and move the dial to the desired temperature of 320oF (Fahrenheit).

- Press the "Start/Pause" button on your keyboard.

- When the machine beeps to indicate that it has been warmed, remove the cover and set it aside.

- Place the pan on top of the "Wire Rack" in the oven.

- Meanwhile, in a separate dish, whisk together the eggs until thoroughly combined.

- Mix in the parsley until everything is well-combined.

- After 6 minutes of cooking, evenly spread the egg mixture on top of the ham.

- Cut the wedges into equal-sized pieces and place them on a plate.

Nutrition:

- Total fat: 15.5 g Saturated fat: 5.3 g Calories: 228 Total fat: 15.5 g Saturated fat: 5.3 g

- 270 milligrams of cholesterol

- Sodium: 608 milligrams Carbohydrates in total: 3.5 g 0.9 g of dietary fiber

- 2.1 g of sugar

- 19.8 grams of protein

Frittata with turkey, spinach, and broccoli.

Time required for preparation: 30 minutes 4 portions (servings)

Ingredients:

- 1 tablespoon extra-virgin olive oil

- cut into tiny pieces 6 turkey sausage links (from the turkey) 1 cup broccoli florets, chopped into small pieces (about 1 cup total)

- 1/2 cup fresh spinach, finely chopped 6 eggs 1 tablespoon hot sauce

- garlic salt (half and half tsp.), 2 tablespoons

- Season with salt and freshly ground black pepper as needed.

Directions:

- In a pan, heat the olive oil over medium heat and cook the sausage for about 7-8 minutes or until it is browned on both sides.

- Cook for approximately 3-4 minutes after adding the broccoli.

- Cook for approximately 2-3 minutes after adding the spinach.

- Remove the pan from the heat and set it aside to cool for a few minutes.

- Between batches, combine the eggs, half-and-half, hot sauce, garlic salt, salt, and freshly ground black pepper in a large mixing bowl. Beat until thoroughly blended.

- The broccoli mixture should be placed in the bottom of a lightly oiled baking pan, followed by the egg mixture.

- To choose the "Air Bake" mode, press the "Power Button" on the Air Fry Oven and turn the dial to the right.

- Cooking time may be changed to 15 minutes by pressing the Time button and turning the clock a second time.

- Now, press the Temp button and adjust the dial to the 400oF setting to complete the process.

- Press the "Start/Pause" button on your keyboard.

- When the machine beeps to indicate that it has been warmed, open the oven door and place the food inside. Make sure to serve it hot.

- Place the pan on top of the "Wire Rack" and close the door.

- When you're finished, cut the pieces into equal-sized wedges.

Nutrition:

- Total fat: 27.4 g Saturated fat: 11.6 g Calories: 339 Total fat: 27.4 g

- 229 milligrams of cholesterol

- Sodium: 596 milligrams Carbohydrates in total: 3.7 g Fiber in total: 0.7 g

- 1.5 g of sugar

- 19.6 grams of protein

Frittata de Trout.

Time required for preparation: 25 minutes 4 portions (servings)

Ingredients:

- 1 tablespoon extra-virgin olive oil 1 onion, thinly sliced

- 6 quail eggs

- 1/2 tablespoon of horseradish sauce crème Fraiche (about 2 tablespoons)

- trout fillets that have been hot-smoked and chopped

- 1/4 cup finely chopped fresh dill

Directions:

- The onion should be cooked for around 4-5 minutes in a pan with medium heat and oil added.

- Take the pan off the heat and set it aside.

- Meanwhile, in a large mixing bowl, combine the eggs, horseradish sauce, and crème Fraiche until thoroughly combined.

- Placing the fried onion in the bottom of a baking pan, then topping it with the egg mixture and finishing with the fish, is a good idea.

- To choose the "Air Fry" mode, press the "Power Button" on the Air Fry Oven and turn the dial to the right.

- Cooking time may be changed to 20 minutes by pressing the Time button and turning the dial a second time.

- You may raise or lower the temperature to 320 degrees Fahrenheit by pressing and holding down the Temp button.

- Press the "Start/Pause" button on your keyboard.

- When the machine beeps to indicate that it has been warmed, remove the cover and set it aside.

- Place the pan on top of the "Wire Rack" in the oven to bake.

- As soon as you are finished, cut the chicken into equal-sized pieces and serve with dill garnish.

Nutrition:

- Calories in a serving: 339 Total fat: 27.4 g Saturated fat: 11.6 g Total fat: 27.4 g

- 229 milligrams of cholesterol

- Sodium: 596 milligrams Carbohydrates in total: 3.7 g 0.7 g of dietary fiber

- 1.5 g of sugar

- 19.6 grams of protein

Delicious Potato Hash.

Time required for preparation: 25 minutes 4 portions (servings)

Ingredients:

- 1-1/2 potatoes, diced 1 yellow onion, chopped 2 tbsp. extra-virgin olive oil, to taste

- 1 green bell pepper, peeled and diced, season with salt and black pepper to taste

- 1/2 tsp. Dried thyme (optional) 2 quail eggs

Directions:

- Preheat your air fryer to 350 degrees Fahrenheit, add the oil, heat it, then add the onion, bell pepper, salt, and pepper, stirring constantly, and cook for 5 minutes.

- Combine the potatoes, thyme, and eggs in a large mixing bowl.

- Cook for 20 minutes at 360 degrees Fahrenheit after stirring and covering the pan.

- Divide the mixture among the dishes and serve it for breakfast.

- Enjoy!

Nutrition:

Calories consumed: 241 4 g of fat Fiber:7g Carbohydrates: 1/2 g 7 g of protein

Burrito de Turkey (Turkey Burrito).

Preparation time: 10 minutes Ingredients: Ingredients: Servings: 2

- 4 slices of turkey breast that has previously been cooked

- 1/2 red bell pepper, thinly cut, and 2 eggs

- 2 tablespoons of a small avocado, peeled, pitted, and sliced salsa

- season with salt and freshly ground black pepper to taste,a cup of mozzarella cheese, and grated Tortillas for use in the kitchen

Directions:

- In a large mixing bowl, whisk together the eggs with salt and pepper to taste. Pour the eggs into a pan and set it in the air fryer's basket to cook.

- Cook for 5 minutes at 400 degrees Fahrenheit, remove the pan from the fryer and transfer the eggs to a dish.

- Arrange tortillas on a work surface and divide eggs among them. Divide turkey meat, bell pepper, cheese, salsa, and avocado among the tortillas as evenly as possible.

- After you've prepared your air fryer with tin foil, roll your burritos and set them in the air fryer to cook.

- Heat the burritos for 3 minutes at 300 degrees F before dividing them among plates and serving them.

- Enjoy!

Nutrition:

- Calorie count: 349 23 g of fat Fiber:11g Carbohydrates: 20g 21 g of protein

Oatmeal Casserole

Time required for preparation: 10 minutes. Preparation time: 20 minutes. There are 8 servings in total.

Ingredients:

- 2 cups rolled oats (or equivalent)

- 1-tablespoon baking powder

- 1 / 3 cup granulated sugar

- 1 teaspoon ground cinnamon

- 1/2 cup chocolate chips (optional)

- a third of a cup of blueberries

- 1 banana that has been peeled and mashed

- 2 quarts of milk, a few tablespoons of egg whites, a pat of margarine 1 teaspoon of pure vanilla essence. Using cooking spray

Directions:

- In a large mixing bowl, stir the sugar, baking powder, cinnamon, chocolate chips, blueberries, and banana.

- In a separate dish, whisk together the eggs, vanilla extract, and margarine until well combined.

- Preheat your air fryer to 320 degrees Fahrenheit, oil it with cooking spray, and sprinkle oats on the bottom.

- Cook for 20 minutes after adding the cinnamon mixture and the egg mixture.

- Repeat the process one more time, then divide the mixture among the bowls and serve for breakfast.

- Enjoy!

Nutrition:

- calorie count: 300 4 g of fat Fiber:7g Carbohydrates: 1/2 g

- 10 g of protein

Sweet Potato Hash with a Spicy Kick.

Preparation time: 16 minutes 4 portions (servings)

Ingredients:

- Cook 2 big sweet potatoes till soft and cube them 2 slices ham, cooked and sliced, 2 tablespoons extra-virgin olive oil

- 1 tablespoon of smoked paprika 1 teaspoon of sea salt

- 1 teaspoon freshly ground black pepper 1 teaspoon dried dill weed

Directions:

- In the Air Fry basket, combine the sweet potato, spices, and the olive oil.

- Close the lid of the Air Fryer toaster oven after placing the Air Fryer basket within it.

- Select the Air Fry mode at 400oF for 16 minutes at a temperature of 400oF.

- Every 5 minutes, toss the potatoes to ensure even cooking. Once the pasta is finished, add the ham and serve immediately.

Nutrition:

- Calories in a serving: 134 6.6 g of protein Carbohydrates: 36.5 g 6 g of fat

Hash with potatoes and jalapenos.

Preparation time: 24 minutes 4 portions (servings)

Ingredients:

- Potatoes (peeled and chopped) weighing 1/2 lbs. 1 tablespoon extra-virgin olive oil

- 1 red bell pepper, seeded and chopped (about) 1 small onion, peeled and sliced

- seeds and diced 1 jalapeno (optional)

- 1/2 tbsp. extra-virgin olive oil

- 1/2-tablespoon taco seasoning blend

- 1/2 tsp. cumin seeds, crushed

- Season with salt and freshly ground black pepper to taste

Directions:

- For 20 minutes, soak the potato cubes in cold water, then drain the water.

- Toss the potatoes with 1 tablespoon of extra-virgin olive oil. They should be spread out in the Air Fryer basket. Close the lid of the Air Fryer toaster oven after placing the Air Fryer basket within it. Select the Air Fry setting at 370oF for 18 minutes at that temperature.

- In the meantime, mix the onion, pepper, olive oil, taco seasoning, and the remaining ingredients in a large salad bowl.

- Return the Air Fryer basket with the vegetable mixture to the oven for another 15 minutes. Cook for another 6 minutes at 356 degrees Fahrenheit. Warm the dish before serving.

Nutrition:

- Calories: 242 per serving 8.9 g of protein Carbohydrates: 36.8g 1/4.4 g of fat

Breakfast with Spinach and Eggs.

Preparation time: 20 minutes 4 portions (servings)

- 3 eggs are required for this recipe.

- 15 tablespoons heavy cream; 1/4 cup skimmed milk; 1/4 cup parmesan cheese; 4 ounces spinach; 3 ounces cottage cheese

Directions:

- Preheat the air fryer to 350 degrees Fahrenheit.

- In a large mixing bowl, whisk the eggs, milk, half of the parmesan cheese, and cottage cheese until thoroughly combined. Stir in the spinach until it is evenly distributed.

- Pour the mixture into the baking dish for the air fryer.

- On top, sprinkle the remaining half of the parmesan cheese.

- Cook the meal in the air fryer for 20 minutes at 350 degrees.

- Prepare the dish and serve it.

Nutrition:

- Calories in a serving: 1/44
- 8.5 g of fat
- 2.5 grams of carbohydrates
  o g of sugar
- 1/4 g of protein
- Cholesterol level: 135 milligrams

Vegetable Quiche.

- Preparation time: 24 minutes Ingredients: 6 servings Servings: 6

- 8 quail eggs
- 1 cup skimmed milk (optional)

- 1 cup chopped tomatoes 1 cup chopped zucchini 1 tbsp. Margarine 1 tbsp. Chopped onion 1 tsp. Pepper 1 tbsp. Margarine 1 tbsp. margarine 1 teaspoon of salt

Directions:

- Preheat the air fryer to 370 degrees Fahrenheit.

- Put the olive oil in a pan over medium heat and add the onion, cooking until the onion is gently browned.

- Add the tomatoes and zucchini to the pan and cook for 4-5 minutes or until the tomatoes are soft.

- Transfer the cooked veggies to the baking dish of the air fryer.

- Whisk together the eggs, cheese, milk, pepper, and salt in a large mixing bowl.

- In a baking dish, pour the egg mixture over the veggies.

- Place the eggs in a shallow baking dish and heat for 24 minutes or until the eggs are set.

- Cut into slices and serve.

Nutrition:

- Calories in a serving: 255

- 16 g of fat

- 8 grams of carbohydrates

- 4.2 g of sugar

- 21 g of protein

- 257 milligrams of cholesterol

Tomato and Eggs for Breakfast

Preparation time: 24 minutes Ingredients: Ingredients: Servings: 2

- 2 quail eggs
- 2 big, ripe, organic tomatoes
- 1 tbsp. chopped fresh parsley
- Pepper\Salt

Directions:

- Preheat the air fryer to 325 degrees Fahrenheit.
- Remove the top of a tomato and use a spoon to scoop out the tomato insides. Break one egg into each tomato and place them in the air fryer basket. Cook for 24 minutes or until the egg is set.

- Toss the chicken with parsley, pepper, and salt before serving. Prepare the dish and serve it.

Nutrition:

- 95 calories per serving
- 5 g of fat
- The following are the carbohydrate grams: 7.5 grams
- 5.1 g of sugar
- 7 g of protein
- 164 milligrams of cholesterol

Frittata with Mushrooms and Leek.

Preparation time: 32 minutes 4 portions (servings)

- 6 eggs are required for this recipe.

- 6 ounces of chopped mushrooms 1 cup of thinly sliced leeks

- Salt

Directions:

- Preheat the air fryer to 325 degrees Fahrenheit.

- Prepare a baking dish for the air fryer by spraying it with cooking spray and setting it aside.

- Another pan should be heated over medium heat. Cooking spray should be used on the pan.

- Cook for 6 minutes after adding the mushrooms, leeks, and salt to a pan.

- Break the eggs into a bowl and whisk vigorously.

- Place the sautéed mushroom and leek mixture into the baking dish that has been prepared.

- Pour the egg mixture over the mushroom mixture.

- Cook for 32 minutes in an air fryer after placing the dish in it.

- Prepare the dish and serve it.

Nutrition:

- Calories in a serving: 116

- 7 g of fat

- Carbohydrates: 5.1 g Sugar: 2.1 g

Nutritional Information

- 10 g of protein

- 245 milligrams of cholesterol

Cauliflower from India.

Preparation time: 20 minutes Ingredients: Ingredients: Servings: 2

- 3 cups cauliflower florets (or whatever size you like) 2 tablespoons of water

- 2 teaspoons freshly squeezed lemon juice

- 1/2 tablespoons ginger paste 1 teaspoon of chili powder

- 1/4 tbsp. ground turmeric

- 1/2 cup vegetable stock (optional)

- Pepper\Salt

Directions:

- Combine the ingredients in a baking dish placed in the air fryer and stir thoroughly.

- Cook the meal for 10 minutes at 400 degrees Fahrenheit in an air fryer.

- Cook for another 10 minutes at 360 degrees Fahrenheit after thoroughly stirring.

- Stir well before serving.

Nutrition:

Calories in a serving: 49

- 0.5 g of fat

- 9 grams of carbohydrates

- 3 g of sugar

- 3 g of protein

- Cholesterol: 0 milligrams

Banana Oats are a delicious breakfast option.

Preparation time: 20 minutes Ingredients: 4 servings (servings per recipe)

- 2 cups rolled oats (old-fashioned)

- Sugar (about 13 cups) 1 teaspoon vanilla essence

- 1 banana, peeled and mashed (about 1 cup) 2 cups almond milk, stir together 2 eggs Using cooking spray

Directions:

- In a large mixing basin, whisk the oats, sugar, and other ingredients (excluding the cooking spray) until well combined.

- Preheat your air fryer to 340 degrees Fahrenheit and coat it with frying spray. Add the oats mix and stir it about before covering it and cooking it for 20 minutes.

- Divide the mixture between the two dishes and serve for breakfast.

Nutrition:

- 260 calories per serving
- 4 g of fat 7 g of dietary fiber Carbohydrates: 9 g
- 10 g of protein

Salad de Zucchini.

Time required for preparation: 25 minutes 4 portions (servings)

Ingredients:

- 1 pound of zucchini, sliced into thin slices

2 tablespoons of tomato paste

- Tarragon (1/2 tablespoons), finely minced 1 yellow squash, sliced 1/2 lb. carrots, peeled and chopped 1 tbsp. extra-virgin olive oil

- Seasonings (pepper, salt, etc.)

Directions:

- Combine the zucchini, tomato paste, tarragon, squash, carrots, pepper, and salt in a baking dish placed in the air fryer. Drizzle with a little extra virgin olive oil.

- Place the ingredients in an air fryer and cook at 400oF for 25 minutes until crispy. Halfway through, give it a good stir.

- Prepare the dish and serve it.

Nutrition:

- 79 calories per serving

- 3 g of fat

- 11 g of carbohydrate calories

- 5 g of sugar

- 2 g of protein

Pumpkin Oatmeal.

Preparation time: 3 minutes Recipe makes 1 serving. Ingredients:

- 1/4 cup rolled oats, 1 teaspoon cinnamon

- 1/2 cup pumpkin puree (optional) a pinch of freshly grated ginger Using a pinch of ground cloves

- 1/2 cup plain cottage cheese (no salt added) 1 tbsp. Sugar Baking combination made with Truvia

Direction:

- In a microwave-safe dish or bowl, combine all ingredients except the cheese.

- Make a thorough mix.

- Microwave on high for 80 to 90 seconds, depending on your microwave.

- Toss in the cottage cheese. 1 minute on high power in the microwave

- Refrigerate for up to 1 day after storing in a glass jar with a tight-fitting cover.

Nutrition:

- Calories in a serving: 205

- 3 g of fat

- 3 milligrams of cholesterol

- Sodium: 31/2 milligrams

- Amount of carbohydrate (34 g) 7 g of dietary fiber 9 g of sugar

- 1/4 g of protein

Cottage Cheese Pancakes

Preparation time: 5 minutes 4 portions (servings)

Ingredients:

- 1/2 teaspoon baking soda

- 13 cups unbleached all-purpose flour

- 1 cup cottage cheese (low-fat or nonfat) 1/2 tbsp. Oil

- 3 eggs, lightly beaten

- Directions:

- In a large mixing basin, combine all ingredients except the oil.

- Heat the oil in a skillet over medium heat.

- The batter should be stored in a food container.

- Refrigerate until ready to use in the kitchen.

- Pour the batter into the pan when you're ready to start cooking.

- Once the bubbles emerge, flip the card.

- Cook for 2 to 3 minutes or until the potatoes are firm.

Nutrition:

- Calories in a serving: 152

- 7 g of fat

- Cholesterol: 2 milligrams
- Carbohydrate content: 10 g
- Sodium: 385 milligrams
- 2 g of sugar
- 13 g of protein

Breakfast Enchilada (Spanish for "breakfast casserole").

Preparation time: 3 minutes Ingredients: 1 serving (serves 1)

- 1 egg white, beaten until stiff
- 1 egg, lightly beaten Using cooking spray
- season with salt and pepper to taste

- Cubed 1 oz. tofu, cooked according to package directions, 2 tablespoons of salsa

- 1 tablespoon shredded low-fat Mexican cheese (optional)

Direction:

- In a separate dish, whisk together the egg white and the egg.

- Oil should be sprayed into a pan.

- Heat the pan over a medium heat setting.

- Cook for 1 to 2 minutes, without stirring, after which add the eggs.

- Season with salt and freshly ground pepper.

- Cook for another 1 minute on the other side.

- Place on a serving dish.

- Cook the eggs on the other side for approximately 2 minutes, or until they are completely cooked, and then transfer them to a serving platter to cool.

- To finish, add tofu and cheese on top of the egg.

- It's time to roll it up.

- Keep it in a food-safe container.

- Refrigerate for up to 1 day before serving.

- When you're ready to serve, reheat the dish.

- Toss with salsa before serving.

Nutrition:

- Calories: 171 per serving

- 8 g of fat

- Cholesterol: 0 milligrams

- Carbohydrate content: 3 g

- 23 g of protein

- Sodium: 432 milligrams

- 3 g of sugar

Egg Muffins are delicious.

Preparation time: 20 minutes 1/2 servings (about).

Ingredients:

- Using cooking spray

- turkey bacon slices, cooked and split into 1/2 pieces 1/2 cup almond milk 6 eggs, lightly beaten

- a quarter-cup of low-fat Swiss cheese

- 1 / 4 tsp. seasoning with Italian herbs and spices season with salt and pepper to taste

Direction:

- Oil a muffin tin and set aside.

- Preheat your oven to 350 degrees Fahrenheit.

- Bacon should be placed in the muffin cups.

- Combine the remaining ingredients in a large mixing basin.

- Fill the muffin cups halfway with the mixture.

- Preheat the oven to 200°F and bake for 20 minutes.

- Remove egg muffins from the oven and place them in a food storage container.

- Refrigerate for up to 1 day before serving.

- Before serving, reheat the dish.

Nutrition:

- Calories in one serving: 98

- 7 g of fat Cholesterol: 7 milligrams 1 gram of carbohydrates Fiber:0g

- 1 gram of sugar

- 8 g of protein

Spinach & Cottage Cheese Baked in the Oven

Time required for preparation: 30 minutes

Ingredients: 8 servings (serves 8)

- 2 cups cottage cheese (non-fat optional) 2 eggs, lightly beaten

- 10 ounces of spinach

Direction:

- Preheat the oven to 350 degrees Fahrenheit.

- In a large mixing basin, combine the cheese, eggs, and spinach.

- Pour the mixture into a baking pan.

- Preheat the oven to 300°F and bake for 30 minutes.

- Place in a food container and place in the refrigerator.

Nutrition:

- 78 calories per serving

- 3 g of fat

- Cholesterol: 0 milligrams

- There are 3 grams of carbohydrates in total.

- 1 gram of dietary fiber

- 2 g of sugars

- 11 g of protein

Scrambled Broccoli and Tofu with Garlic.

Preparation time: 10 minutes Ingredients: 6 servings Servings: 6

- 1 tablespoon of extra-virgin olive oil

- 11/2 pound tofu, cut into cubes 1 onion, chopped 1/4 pounds mushrooms, chopped 1/2 pounds broccoli, chopped 1 1/2pounds tofu, sliced into cubes 3 eggs, lightly beaten

Direction:

- Preheat your oven to 350 degrees Fahrenheit.

- Heat the oil in a pan over medium heat until shimmering.

- Cook for 1 minute with the onion and mushrooms.

- Push to one side of the room.

- Toss in the tofu and broccoli.

- Cook until the tofu cubes are golden brown, about 10 minutes.

- Combine the mixture and the eggs in a mixing dish.

- Return the egg mixture to the pan and cook for another minute or two.

- Continue to cook until the eggs are set.

- Place in a food container and place in the refrigerator.

Nutrition:

- 78 calories per serving

- 3 g of fat

- Cholesterol: 0 milligrams

- There are 3 grams of carbohydrates in total.

- 1 gram of dietary fiber

- 2 g of sugars

- 11 g of protein

Baked Eggs with Broccoli

Ingredients: 8 servings (serves 8)

- 1 tablespoon extra-virgin olive oil 1/2 cup mushrooms, sliced 10-ounce broccoli florets, chopped 1 teaspoon paprika 6 eggs, beaten 1/2 cup mushrooms, sliced

- season with salt and pepper to taste

Direction:

- Preheat your oven to 350 degrees Fahrenheit.

- In a large mixing basin, combine all of the ingredients.

- Fill a baking pan halfway with the mixture.

- In a preheated oven, bake for 1 hour and 30 minutes.

- Refrigerate after storing in an airtight container.

- Before serving, reheat the dish.

Nutrition:

- 115 calories per serving

- 5 g of fat

- Cholesterol: 75 milligrams

- Carbohydrate content: 5 g

- 419 milligrams of sodium

- 2 g of sugar

- 1/2 g of protein

Egg Cups

Preparation time: 9 minutes Ingredients: Ingredients: Servings: 2

- 3 gently beaten eggs (optional)

- 4 slices of tomato

- 4 tablespoons crumbled cheddar cheese

- 2 bacon pieces, fried till crispy and crumbled Pepper\Salt

Direction:

- Cooking spray should be sprayed onto silicone muffin molds before baking. Whisk together the egg, pepper, and salt in a small mixing bowl. Preheat the air fryer to 350 degrees Fahrenheit.

- Fill the silicone muffin tins halfway with eggs. Molds may be made by dividing the cheese and bacon into them. Place each one in the air fryer basket with a tomato slice on top of it.

- Cook for 9 minutes on medium heat. Prepare the dish and serve it.

Nutrition:

- Calories in a serving: 67

- 4 g of fat

- 1 gram of carbohydrate

- Sugar content: 0.7 g

- Protein content: 5.1 g

- 1/25 milligrams of cholesterol

Pumpkin Pancakes

Preparation time: 1/2 minutes 2 portions (servings)

Ingredients:

- 1 square puff pastry
- 3 tablespoons of pumpkin puree
- 1-egg (small), lightly beaten

Directions:

- Puff pastry should be rolled out into a square and layered with pumpkin pie filling, leaving a 1/4-inch border around the borders of the pie. Cut it into 8 equal-sized square pieces and brush the edges with a beaten egg to seal in the moisture.
- To choose the "Air Fry" mode, press the "Power Button" on the Air Fry Oven and turn the dial to the right. To adjust the cooking time to 1/2

minute, press the Time button twice more and spin the dial.

- Now press the Temp button and turn the dial to 355 degrees Fahrenheit to complete the setting. Finally, press the "Start/Pause" button on your keyboard.

- When the machine beeps to indicate that it has been warmed, remove the cover and set it aside. Place the squares in a "Sheet Pan" that has been oiled and place it in the oven. Warm the dish before serving.

Nutrition:

- Total fat: 6.7 g Saturated fat: 1.8 g Calories: 109 Total fat: 109 Saturated fat: 1.8 g

- Cholesterol: 34 milligrams

- Sodium: 87 milligrams Carbohydrates total: 9.8 g 0.5 g of dietary fiber 2.6 g of sugar

- 2.4 g of protein per serving

Shrimp Frittata.

Preparation time: 15 minutes Ingredients: Ingredients: Servings: 2

- 4 quail eggs

- 1/2 tbsp. basil leaves, dried Using cooking spray

- season with salt and black pepper to taste

- 1/2 cup rice, drained and cooked

- 1/2 cup cooked shrimp, peeled, deveined, and diced (optional)

- 1/2 cup finely chopped baby spinach

- 1/2 cup grated Monterey jack cheese (optional)

Directions:

- Whisk together the eggs, salt, pepper, and basil in a large mixing bowl. Cooking spray should coat the pan of your air fryer before adding the rice, shrimp, and spinach. Cook for 10 minutes at 350oF in your air fryer with the egg mixture and cheese sprinkled all over the top.

- Divide the mixture among the dishes and serve it for breakfast. Enjoy!

Nutrition:

- 162 calories per serving, 6 g of fat Fiber:5g Carbohydrates: 8g 4 g of protein

Sandwiches with tuna.

Preparation time: 5 minutes Ingredients: Ingredients: Servings: 2

- 16 ounces canned tuna, drained 1/4 cup mayonnaise (optional) 2 tablespoons mustard 1 tablespoon lemon juice

- 2 green onions, finely chopped 3 English muffins, half 3 tablespoons butter

- 6 slices of provolone cheese

Directions:

- Stir the tuna, mayonnaise, lemon juice, mustard, and green onions in a large mixing basin.

- Muffin halves should be greased with butter and placed in an air fryer that has been warmed to 350oF for 4 minutes before serving.

- Spread the tuna mixture over the muffin halves and top each with a slice of provolone cheese. Place the sandwiches back in the air fryer for 4 minutes, divide them among plates and serve them for breakfast immediately. Enjoy!

Nutrition:

- Calories in this recipe: 182 4 g of fat Fiber:7g Carbohydrates: 8g 6 g of protein

Sandwiches with shrimp.

Preparation time: 5 minutes 2 portions (servings)

Ingredients:

- 1 and 1/4 cups shredded cheddar cheese

- 1 can of small shrimp (drained) (about 6 ounces) 3 tablespoons of mayonnaise

- 2 tablespoons finely sliced green onions 4 pieces of whole wheat bread, toasted

- 2 tablespoons melted butter (softened)

Directions:

- In a large mixing bowl, combine the shrimp, cheese, green onion, and mayonnaise. Stir thoroughly. Smear half of the bread slices with this mixture, top with the other half of the bread pieces, cut in half diagonally and spread the remaining butter.

- Place the sandwiches in your air fryer and cook for 5 minutes at 350 degrees Fahrenheit. Serve the shrimp sandwiches for breakfast on plates divided in half. Enjoy!

Nutrition:

- 162 calories per serving, 3 g of fat Fiber:7g Carbohydrates: 1/2 g 4 g of protein

Omelet with chicken and zucchini.

Preparation time: 35 minutes Ingredients: Ingredients: Servings: 2

- 8 quail eggs
- 1/2 cup whole milk
- Season with salt and freshly ground black pepper as needed. 1 cup cooked and chopped chicken (optional)
- 1 cup shredded Cheddar cheese (optional)
- 1/2 cup finely chopped fresh chives 3/4 cups finely chopped zucchini

Directions:

- In a large mixing bowl, whisk together the eggs, milk, salt, and black pepper until thoroughly combined. Stir in the other ingredients until everything is well-combined.

- Pour the mixture into a baking pan that has been buttered. To choose the "Air Bake" mode, press the "Power Button" on the Air Fry Oven and turn the dial to the right.

- To adjust the cooking time to 35 minutes, press the "Time" button twice and spin the dial. Now, press the Temp button and adjust the dial to the 315oF setting to complete the process.

- Press the "Start/Pause" button on your keyboard. When the machine beeps to indicate that it has been warmed, remove the cover and set it aside. Place the pan on top of the "Wire Rack" in the oven. Serve immediately after cutting into equal-sized wedges.

Nutrition:

- calories: 209 total fat: 13.3 g saturated fat: 6.3 g total fat calories: 209

- 258 milligrams of cholesterol

- Sodium: 252 milligrams Carbohydrates in total: 2.3 g 0.3 g of dietary fiber

- 1.8 g of sugar

- 9.8 grams of protein

Zucchini Fritters

Preparation time: 7 minutes 2 portions (servings)

Ingredients:

- zucchini, shredded and pressed (11 1/2 ounces) Halloumi cheese (about 7)

- 1/4 cup unbleached all-purpose flour 2 quail eggs

- 1 teaspoon finely minced fresh dill

- Season with salt and freshly ground black pepper as needed.

Directions:

- All of the ingredients should be combined in a large mixing dish.

- Make a small-sized patty out of the remaining ingredients.

- To choose the "Air Fry" mode, press the "Power Button" on the Air Fry Oven and turn the dial to the right.

- Cooking time may be changed to 7 minutes by pressing the Time button and turning the dial a second time.

- Now press the Temp button and turn the dial to 355 degrees Fahrenheit to complete the temperature setting process.

- Press the "Start/Pause" button on your keyboard.

- When the machine beeps to indicate that it has been warmed, remove the cover and set it aside.

- Place the patties in a greased "Sheet Pan" and bake for 15 minutes at 350°F.

- When the dish is finished, it should be served warm.

Nutrition:

- 253 calories total fat 17.2 g saturated fat 11 g total fat

- 1/21 milligrams of cholesterol

- Sodium: 333 milligrams Carbohydrates in total: 10 g 1.1 g of fiber, 2.7 g of sugar

- Protein content: 15.2 g

Omelet with onions.

Preparation time: 15 minutes Ingredients: Ingredients: Servings: 2

- 4 quail eggs

- 1/4 teaspoon low-sodium soy sauce (optional) Depending on how much is needed, freshly ground black pepper, 1 tablespoon of melted butter

- 1/4 cup shredded Cheddar cheese 1 medium yellow onion, sliced 1 medium red pepper, sliced

Directions:

- In a pan, melt the butter over medium heat and sauté the onion for about 8-10 minutes, until the onion is translucent.

- Remove the pan from the heat and set it aside to cool for a few minutes.

- In the meantime, combine the eggs, soy sauce, and black pepper in a mixing bowl.

- Gently mix in the sautéed onion until everything is well-combined.

- Place the zucchini mixture on a small baking sheet and bake for 15 minutes. To choose the "Air Fry" mode, press the "Power Button" on the Air Fry Oven and turn the dial to the right.

- Cooking time may be changed to 5 minutes by pressing the Time button and turning the dial a second time.

- Now press the Temp button and turn the dial to 355 degrees Fahrenheit to complete the setting. Finally, press the "Start/Pause" button on your keyboard.

- When the machine beeps to indicate that it has been warmed, remove the cover and set it aside.

- Place the pan on top of the "Wire Rack" in the oven.

- Wait until the omelet is finished, divide it into two parts and serve it hot.

Nutrition:

- The total fat content is 15.4 g, with 6.9 g of saturated fat. The calories are 222.

- 347 milligrams of cholesterol

- Sodium: 264 milligrams Carbohydrates in total: 6.1 g 1.2 g of dietary fiber 3.1 g of sugar

- Protein content: 15.3 g

Tortilla de Peas para el Desayuno.

Preparation time: 7 minutes Ingredients: Ingredients: Servings: 2

- 1/2 pound of baby peas 4 tablespoons butter and 1/2 cup plain yogurt 8 quail eggs

- 1/2 cup mint leaves, finely chopped

- season with salt and black pepper to taste

Directions:

- Heat the butter in a large skillet to accommodate your air fryer over medium heat before adding the peas.

- Cook for a couple of minutes while stirring constantly.

- In the meantime, mix half of the yogurt with the salt, pepper, eggs, and mint in a large mixing bowl.

- Pour this over the peas and stir well before placing them in the air fryer and cooking for 7 minutes at 350oF.

- Spread the remaining yogurt over your tortilla, slice it, and serve it immediately. Enjoy!

Nutrition:

- 192 calories per serving, 5 g of fat Fiber:4g Carbohydrates: 8 g

- 7 g of protein

Chicken with an almond crust.

Time required for preparation: 25 minutes

Ingredients: Ingredients: Servings: 2

- 2 chicken breasts, skinless and boneless, cooked in a skillet

- Dijon mustard

- 2 tablespoons of mayonnaise

- 1/4 cup blanched almonds Pepper\Salt

Directions:

- Place the almonds in a food processor and pulse until they are coarsely chopped.

- Place the almonds on a platter and leave them away for now.

- Combine the mustard and mayonnaise in a small bowl and distribute over the chicken.

- Cook the chicken at 350oF for 25 minutes after coating it with almond paste and placing it in an air fryer basket.

- Prepare the dish and serve it.

Nutrition:

- Calories in a serving: 409

- 22 g of fat

- carbohydrate grammage: 6 grammage

- 1.5 g of sugar

- 45 g of protein

- 134 milligrams of cholesterol

Breakfast Fish Tacos (Fish Tacos for Breakfast).

Preparation time: 13 minutes Ingredients: Ingredients: Servings: 2

- 4 large flour tortillas

- 1 red bell pepper, finely diced 1 small yellow onion, finely sliced 1 cup cooked corn

- skinless and boneless white fish fillets (four fillets)

- 1/2 cup of salsa

- Mix romaine lettuce, spinach, and radicchio in a large bowl. Add 4 tablespoons of grated parmesan cheese.

Directions:

- Cook the fish fillets for 6 minutes at 350 degrees Fahrenheit in your air fryer.

- Meanwhile, heat a skillet over medium-high heat and add the bell pepper, onion, and corn. Cook until the vegetables are tender.

- Cook for 1-2 minutes, stirring constantly.

- Place tortillas on a work surface, split fish fillets among them, pour salsa over them, divide mixed vegetables and greens, and sprinkle parmesan cheese over each after the process.

- Roll your tacos and throw them in an air fryer preheated to 350 degrees Fahrenheit for 6 minutes longer.

- Serve the fish tacos for breakfast by dividing them among plates. Enjoy!

Nutrition:

- Calories in a serving: 200 3 g of fat, 7 g of dietary fiber, 9 g of carbohydrates, 5 g of protein.

Chapter Three

Lunch

Greek Lamb Chops.

Time required for preparation: 10 minutes

Ingredients: 4 servings (servings per recipe)

- lamb chops weighing 2 lbs.

- 2 tablespoons minced garlic 1 1/2 tsp. oregano leaves, dried

- 1/4 cup freshly squeezed lemon juice

- 1/4 cup extra-virgin olive oil

- 1/2 tsp. black pepper 1 teaspoon of salt

Directions:

- In a large mixing basin, combine the lamb chops. Pour the remaining ingredients over the lamb chops and toss to coat well.

- Place the lamb chops on the air fryer oven tray and cook for 5 minutes at 400 degrees Fahrenheit.

- Cook for another 5 minutes after turning the lamb chops.

Prepare the dish and serve it.

- Nutrition:

- Calories in a serving: 538

- 29.4 g of fat

- Carbohydrates: 1.3 g

- 64 g of protein

Roasted Beef

Preparation time: 45 minutes 6 individual servings

Ingredients: 2 1/2 lbs. beef roast, 2 tbsp. Brown sugar, 2 tbsp. seasoning with Italian herbs and spices

Directions:

- Prepare the roast by placing it on the rotisserie spite.

- After seasoning the roast with Italian seasoning, place it in the instant vortex air fryer oven to cook.

- A meat thermometer should register 1/45oF when the beef roast is done, air frying at 350oF for 45 minutes or until the internal temperature of the beef roast is reached.

- Cut into slices and serve.

Nutrition:

- 365 calories are required for this recipe.
- Fat (in grams): 13.2 g
- Carbohydrates: 0.5 g
- Protein content: 57.4 g

Rib-eye Steak with butter sauce.

Preparation time: 1/4 minutes 4 portions (servings)

The following ingredients are needed: 2 pounds bone-in rib eye steak, 1 teaspoon fresh rosemary, chopped 1 teaspoon fresh thyme, chopped 2 teaspoons fresh parsley, chopped 1 teaspoon garlic, minced 1/4 cup softened butter 1 teaspoon fresh oregano, minced 1 teaspoon fresh oregano, minced

1 teaspoon fresh oregano, minced 1 teaspoon fresh oregano, minced Pepper\Salt

Instructions:

- In a small mixing bowl, blend the butter and herbs until well combined.

- 30 minutes before serving, brush herb butter on the rib-eye steak and place it in the refrigerator to marinate.

- Place the marinated steak on an instant vortex air fryer oven pan and cook for 1/2-1/4 minutes at 400 degrees Fahrenheit.

- Prepare the dish and serve it.

Nutrition:

- Calories in a serving: 416

- 36.7 g fat 0.7 g carbohydrate

- Protein content: 20.3 g

Beef Jerky in the traditional sense.

Preparation time: 4 hours 4 portions (servings)

Ingredients:

- 2 pounds London broil, thinly sliced 1 teaspoon of onion powder

- a tablespoon of brown sugar, 3 tablespoons soy sauce

- 1 tablespoon extra-virgin olive oil

- a quarter teaspoon of garlic powder

Directions:

- In a large zip-lock bag, combine all ingredients except the meat.

- Combine until everything is well-combined. Place the meat in the bag.

- Seal the bag and gently massage the meat to ensure that all marinadesare absorbed.

- Allow the meat to marinade for 1 hour.

- Place the marinated beef slices on the instant vortex air fryer tray and dehydrate at 160oF for 4 hours, turning the tray halfway through.

Nutrition:

- Calories in a serving: 133

- 4.7 g of fat

- Carbohydrates: 9.4 g

- Protein (in grams): 13.4 g

Chapter Four

Other Varieties

Season and Salt-Cured Beef.

Preparation time: 3 hours Ingredients: 4 servings (servings per recipe)

- beef round, weighing 1 1/2 pounds, trimmed

- 1/2 cup Worcestershire sauce (optional)

- 1/2 cup soy sauce with a reduced sodium content 2 tablespoons of honey

- 1 teaspoon of liquid smoke 2 tbsp. onion powder (optional)

- 1/2 tsp. Red pepper flakes (optional)

- Depending on how much is needed, freshly ground black pepper

Directions:

- Set the meat in a zip-top bag and place it in the freezer for 1-2 hours to firm up.

- Using a sharp knife, place the meat on a chopping board and cut it into 1/4-inch strips against the grain.

- In a large mixing basin, incorporate the remaining ingredients until everything is well-combined.

- Add the steak pieces and liberally cover them with the sauce mixture.

- Refrigerate for 4-6 hours to allow the flavors to blend.

- Remove the beef slices from the bowl and blot them dry with paper towels to remove any excess moisture.

- Divide the steak strips among the baking pans and put them in an equal layers on the baking trays.

- Select "Dehydrate" from the drop-down menu and set the temperature to 160oF.

- Set the timer for three hours and hit the "Start" button.

- When the display indicates that "Add Food" should be done, place one tray in the top position and another in the middle.

- After 11/2 hours, rotate the cooking trays to a different position.

- Cook for about 10 minutes, stirring in a small saucepan with the remaining ingredients over medium heat until the vegetables are tender.

- Removing the trays from the Vortex once the cooking time is complete is a good idea.

Nutrition:

- calorie count: 372

- 10.7 g of fat

- Carbohydrates: 1/2 g

- Protein (in grams): 53.8 g

Meatballs in a sweet and spicy sauce.

Preparation time: 30 minutes. There are 8 servings in total.

Ingredients:

- For the meatballs, use 1 pound of lean ground beef.
- a third cup of quick-cooking oats
- 1/2 cup Ritz crackers, crumbled 1 (5-ounce) can evaporate milk 1 cup sugar 2 big eggs that have been gently beaten
- 1 teaspoon of honey
- 1 tablespoon finely chopped onion (dry and sliced) Garlic powder (one teaspoon)
- 1 teaspoon cumin seeds, ground
- Season with salt and freshly ground black pepper as needed.
- Sauce (optional):
- 13 cup orange marmalade (optional)
- 13 cup honey (about)

- 1 / 3 cup granulated sugar 2 tablespoons of cornstarch 2 tablespoons soy sauce 1-2 tablespoons of spicy sauce

- 1 tablespoon Worcestershire sauce (optional)

Directions:

- Combine all ingredients in a large mixing basin for the meatballs until thoroughly blended.

- The mixture should be formed into 1 1/2-inch balls.

- Place half the meatballs on a baking sheet and arrange them in a single layer.

- Place the drip pan at the bottom of the Instant Vortex Plus Air Fryer Oven's cooking chamber to catch any drips.

- Using the "Air Fry" option, set the temperature to 380 degrees Fahrenheit.

- Set a timer for 15 minutes and hit the "Start" button to begin.

- When the display indicates that "Add Food" should be done, place the cooking tray in the center of the oven.

- The meatballs should be turned when the display says, "Turn Food."

- Removing the tray from the Vortex is important after the cooking time is complete.

- Then repeat the process with the remaining meatballs.

- Meanwhile, prepare the sauce by combining the ingredients in a small saucepan over medium heat and cooking until thickened, stirring constantly.

- Serve the meatballs with a dollop of the sauce on top.

Nutritional Information:

- 411 calories

- 11.1 g of total fat

- Carbohydrates: 38.8 g

- Protein content: 38.9 g

Pork Shoulder with a Spicy Rub.

Preparation Time: 55 minutes 6 individual servings

Ingredients:

- 1 teaspoon cumin, freshly ground

- 1 tsp. Cayenne pepper (optional) Garlic powder (one teaspoon)

- Season with salt and freshly ground black pepper as needed. 2 lbs. pork shoulder with the skin still on

Directions:

- Combine the spices, salt, and black pepper in a small mixing bowl until well combined.

- Place the pork shoulder on a chopping board, skin-side down, and cut it into pieces.

- Season the interior side of the pork shoulder with salt and black pepper before grilling or roasting.

- Wrap the pork shoulder with kitchen twine and roll it into a long circular cylinder.

- The exterior surface of the pork shoulder should be seasoned with the spice combination.

- Insert the rotisserie rod through the pork shoulder. Remove the rotisserie rod.

- To secure the pork shoulder, place two rotisserie forks on either side of the rod, one on each side.

- Place the drip pan at the bottom of the Instant Vortex Plus Air Fryer Oven's cooking chamber to catch any drips.

- Select "Roast" and then lower the temperature to 350 degrees Fahrenheit.

- Set the timer for 55 minutes and then hit the "Start" button to begin.

- To put the left side of the rod into the Vortex, press the red lever until the display says "Add Food."

- After that, slip the rod's left side into a groove along the metal bar to ensure it does not move.

- Then close the door and press the "Rotate" button.

- As soon as the cooking time is through, press the red lever to release the rod.

- Remove the pork from the Vortex and set it aside on a serving tray for approximately 10 minutes before slicing it up.

- Cut the pork shoulder into desired-sized slices with a sharp knife and arrange it on a serving platter.

Nutrition:

- Calories in a serving: 445

- 32.5 g of fat

- Protein: 35.4 g Carbohydrates: 0.7 g

Seasoned Pork Tenderloin.

Preparation time: 45 minutes Ingredients: 5 servings (serves 5)

- Tenderloin of pork weighing 1/2 lb.

- 2 to 3 tablespoons of spice for bbq pork

Directions:

- Season the pork with a good amount of seasoning. Plunge the rotisserie rod into the pork tenderloin from top to bottom.

- The rotisserie forks should be inserted into the rod on each side to secure the pork tenderloin.

- Place the drip pan at the bottom of the Instant Vortex plus Air Fryer Oven's cooking chamber to catch any drips.

- Select "Roast" and then raise the temperature to 360 degrees Fahrenheit.

- Set the timer for 45 minutes and then hit the "Start" button.

- To put the left side of the rod into the Vortex, press the red lever until the display says "Add Food."

- After that, slip the rod's left side into a groove along the metal bar to ensure it does not move.

- Then close the door and press the "Rotate" button.

- As soon as the cooking time is through, press the red lever to release the rod.

- Remove the pork from the Vortex and set it aside on a serving tray for approximately 10 minutes before slicing it up.

- Using a sharp knife, cut the roast into desired-sized pieces and place them on a serving platter.

Nutrition:

- Calories in this recipe: 195

- 4.8 g of fat

- Carbohydrates: 0 g

- Protein (in grams): 35.6 g

Tenderloin of Pork with Garlic.

- Preparation time: 20 minutes Ingredients: 11/2 lbs. pork tenderloin (serves 5 people). Cooking spray with a nonstick coating

- 2 cloves of roasted garlic, tiny heads

- Season with salt and freshly ground black pepper as needed.

Directions:

- Using cooking spray, lightly coat all sides of the pork with salt and black pepper before seasoning with salt and pepper.

- Rub the meat with the roasted garlic at this point. Prepare the roast by placing it on a baking sheet that has been lightly oiled.

- Place the drip pan at the bottom of the Instant Vortex plus Air Fryer Oven's cooking chamber to catch any drips.

- Select "Air Fry" and raise the temperature to 400 degrees Fahrenheit. Start by setting the timer for 20 minutes and pressing the "Start" button.

- When the display indicates that "Add Food" should be done, place the cooking tray in the center of the oven.

- When the display indicates that the food should be turned, turn the pork.

- Removing the tray from the Vortex and transferring the roast to a dish for roughly 10 minutes before slicing is recommended when cooking time is completed. Then, cut the roast into desired-sized pieces with a sharp knife and arrange it on a serving platter.

Nutrition:

- Calories in a serving: 202
- 4.8 g of fat
- Carbohydrates: 1.7 g
- Protein content: 35.9 g

Pork Tenderloin with a Glaze.

Preparation time: 20 minutes 3 portions (servings)

Ingredients:

- 1 pound of pork tenderloin 2 tablespoons of Sriracha

- 2 tablespoons of honey Sodium chloride, when needed

Directions:

- Plunge the rotisserie rod into the pork tenderloin from top to bottom.

- To attach the pork tenderloin, insert the rotisserie forks into the rod, one on each side of the rod, as shown.

- Combine the Sriracha, honey, and salt in a small mixing bowl until thoroughly combined.

- Coat the pork tenderloin with the honey mixture using a pastry brush.

- Place the drip pan at the bottom of the Instant Vortex Plus Air Fryer Oven's cooking chamber to catch any drips.

- Select "Air Fry" and lower the temperature to 350 degrees Fahrenheit.

- Start by setting the timer for 20 minutes and pressing the "Start" button.

- To put the left side of the rod into the Vortex, press the red lever until the display says "Add Food."

- After that, slip the rod's left side into a groove along the metal bar to ensure it does not move.

- Then close the door and press the "Rotate" button.

- As soon as the cooking time is through, press the red lever to release the rod.

- Remove the pork from the Vortex and set it aside on a serving tray for approximately 10 minutes before slicing it up.

- Using a sharp knife, cut the roast into desired-sized pieces and place them on a serving platter.

Nutrition:

- Calories in a serving: 269

- 5.3 g of total fat

- Carbohydrates: 13.5 g

- Protein content: 39.7 g

Pork Tenderloin in a Country Style.

Time required for preparation: 15 minutes required for preparation: 25 minutes 3 portions (servings)

Ingredients:

- 1 pound of pork tenderloin 1 tablespoon minced garlic 2 tablespoons soy sauce

- 2 tablespoons of honey

- 1 tablespoon of Dijon mustard 1 tablespoon of grain mustard 1 tablespoon of Sriracha sauce

Directions:

- Combine all of the ingredients (except the pork) in a large mixing bowl and combine.

- Combine all ingredients in a large mixing bowl and liberally cover the pork tenderloin.

- Refrigerate for 2-3 hours to allow the flavors to blend.

- Remove the pork tenderloin from the marinade, saving the marinade in a separate container.

- Place the pork tenderloin on a baking sheet that has been lightly oiled.

- Place the drip pan at the bottom of the Instant Vortex Plus Air Fryer Oven's cooking chamber to catch any drips.

- Using the "Air Fry" option, set the temperature to 380 degrees Fahrenheit.

- Set a timer for 25 minutes and hit the "Start" button to begin.

- When the display indicates that "Add Food" should be done, place the cooking tray in the center of the oven.

- When the display indicates "Turn Food," turn the pork and oats with the marinade set aside.

- When cooking is over, remove the tray from the Vortex and let the pork tenderloin rest on a dish for about 10 minutes before slicing it thinly.

- Cut the pork tenderloin into desired-sized pieces with a sharp knife and arrange it on a serving platter.

Nutrition:

- Calories in a serving: 277

- 5.7 g of fat

- Carbohydrates: 1/4.2 g

- Protein content: 40.7 g

Lemony Lentils with "Fried" Onions

Time required for preparation: 30 minutes 4 portions (servings)

Ingredients:

- 1 cup red lentils (optional) 4 quarts of water

- Spraying with cooking oil (sunflower or safflower)

- one onion of medium size, peeled and sliced into 1/4-inch-thick rings Sodium chloride (sea salt)

- 1/2 cup kale, stems removed, finely sliced 1/2 cup spinach minced or pressed 3 big garlic cloves (around 1 pound) 2 tablespoons freshly squeezed lemon juice

- 2 tablespoons nutritional yeast 1 teaspoon of sea salt

- 1 teaspoon freshly grated lemon zest (see Ingredient Tip)

- a quarter teaspoon of freshly ground black pepper

Directions:

- Bring the lentils and water to a boil in a medium-large saucepan over medium-high heat, stirring occasionally. Low-heat simmer for 30 minutes (or until the lentils are completely dissolved), occasionally stirring (to prevent the lentils from sticking to the bottom of the pot) and frequently stirring (to avoid clumping).

- While the lentils are cooking, start putting the remainder of your food on the table. After spraying with oil, the onion rings should be separated as much as possible when they are placed in the air fryer basket. Spray them with oil and sprinkle them with a pinch of salt to taste. Fry for 5 minutes over medium heat. Remove the air fryer basket from the oven, shake or stir it, spray it with oil again, and cook for another 5 minutes at 350°F. To ensure that all the onion slices are crisp and thoroughly browned, remove them from the air fryer basket and place them on a dish as soon as they begin to crisp and brown on their own.

• Remove the air fryer basket from the oven and spritz the onions with oil again. Fry for 5 minutes or until the onions are crisp and browned on all sides.

• The kale should be added last, and it should be thoroughly mixed in because the heat from the lentils will steam the thinly sliced greens. To complete the lentils: Combine the garlic, lemon juice, Nutrition yeast, salt, lemon zest, and pepper in a large mixing bowl. Stir everything up thoroughly before dividing it evenly among the bowls. Serve immediately with the crispy onion rings on top.

Nutrition:

- Calories: 220 total calories

- Fatty acids: 1 g Saturated Fatty acids: 0 g Cholesterol: 0 milligrams 477 milligrams of sodium There are 39 grams of carbohydrates in this recipe. Fiber:16g

- 15 g of protein

Every day Bean.

Preparation time: 8 minutes Ingredients: Ingredients: Servings: 2

- Pinto beans (15 oz. can drained) 1/4 cup tomato sauce (optional)

- 2 tbsp. of the mixture Yeast for nutritional purposes

- 2 big garlic cloves, peeled and crushed or finely chopped

- 1/2 tsp. Dried oregano leaves

- Cumin, 1/4 tsp.

- The main ingredients are sea salt and 1 teaspoon of freshly ground black pepper. Spraying with cooking oil (sunflower, safflower)

Directions:

- Using a medium-sized mixing bowl, thoroughly incorporate the beans, tomato sauce,

Nutrition Yeast, garlic, oregano, cumin, salt, and pepper until evenly distributed.

- After spraying the baking pan with oil and filling it with the bean mixture, bake for 30 minutes at 350 degrees. Preheat the oven to 400°F and bake for 4 minutes.

- Remove the pan from the oven, stir thoroughly, and bake for another 4 minutes or until the mixture has thickened and is thoroughly heated. Almost certainly, a small crust will form on top, and it will be gently browned in certain areas.

- Serve when still heated. This can be kept in the refrigerator for up to a week if stored in an airtight container.

Nutrition:

Total fat: 4g Saturated fat: 1g Calories: 284 Total fat: 1g Saturated fat: 1g Cholesterol: 0 milligrams Sodium: 807 milligrams There are 47 grams of carbohydrates in total.

Fiber:16g 20 g of protein

With Creamy Lime Sauce, make a Taco Salad.

Preparation time: 20 minutes 3 portions (servings)

Ingredients:

- To make the sauce, combine the following ingredients:

- silken-firm tofu (one package, 1/2.3 ounces)

- 1/4 cup + 1 tablespoon freshly squeezed lime juice 1 big lime with the zest removed (1 tsp.)

- 1/2 tablespoon of sugar

- Peeled and minced 3 big garlic cloves 1 teaspoon of sea salt

- 1/2 teaspoon ground chipotle pepper powder

- To make the salad, combine the following ingredients:

- 6 cups of romaine lettuce, finely diced (1 large head)

- 1 (15-ounce) can of vegan beans (refried), drained (or whole pinto or black beans if you prefer)

- cup red cabbage, chopped medium tomatoes, chopped 1/2 cup cilantro, chopped 1/4 cup scallions, minced Ingredients: cup red cabbage, chopped medium tomatoes, chopped

- Tortilla Chips with Garlic and Lime in a Double Batch

Directions:

To prepare the sauce, follow these steps:

- Drain the tofu (and any liquid it may have released) and place it in a blender. Combine the lime juice and zest, coconut sugar, garlic, salt, and chipotle powder in a mixing bowl until well combined. Blend until the mixture is completely smooth. Make a mental note to put it away.

- To prepare the salad, follow these steps:

- Divide the lettuce into three large serving basins in an even distribution.

- Warm the beans in a small saucepan over medium heat, often stirring, until they are hot (this should take less than a minute). Place on top of the lettuce and toss to combine.

- The cabbage, tomatoes, cilantro, and scallions should be placed on top of the beans.

- Drizzle generously with the Creamy Lime Sauce and serve with the second batch of air-fried tortilla chips to complete the meal. Take pleasure in it right away.

Nutrition:

- Calories in total: 422

- 7 g of saturated fat

- 1 gram of fat Cholesterol: 0 milligrams Sodium: 1186 milligrams 71 grams of carbohydrates Fiber:15g

- 22 g of protein

Chimichanga.

Preparation time: 8 minutes Ingredients: whole-grain tortilla (serving size: 1).

- 1/2 cup refried vegan beans (optional)

- vegan cheese, grated (1/4 cup) (optional) Spraying with cooking oil (sunflower, safflower)

- fresh salsa or Green Chili Sauce cups (around 1/2 cup) chopped romaine lettuce (about 1/2 head) Guacamole is a type of avocado sauce (optional)

- Cilantro leaves, finely chopped (optional) Cheesy Dipping Sauce (optional)

Directions:

- Place the beans in the center of the tortilla on a level surface and fold the tortilla over. If using cheese, sprinkle it over the top.

- Wrap the bottom of the pastry around the filling and then fold the sides in. Then fold everything up so the beans are completely encased within the tortilla (you're creating an enclosed burrito here).

- Then spray the top of the chimichanga with oil after placing it in the air fryer basket with the seam-side down.

- Fry for 5 minutes over medium heat. Spray the top (as well as the sides) with oil a second time, flip the piece over and spray the other side with oil. Fry for 2 or 3 minutes or until the potatoes are beautifully browned and crisp.

- Place on a serving dish. Season the top of each taco with salsa and/or guacamole (if using), cilantro (if using), and/or Cheesy Sauce (if using). Serve as soon as possible.

Nutrition:

317 calories, 6 grams of total fat

2 g of Saturated Fatty Acids Cholesterol: 0 milligrams Sodium: 955 milligrams 55 g of carbohydrates Fiber:11g

13 g of protein

Crust: Cilantro Lime Cornmeal Crust with Tamale Filling.

Preparation time: 20 minutes 4 portions (servings)

Ingredients:

- For the filling, use the following ingredients:

- 3/4 pound medium zucchini, diced (1 1/4 cups)

- 2 tbsp. oil with no discernible taste (sunflower, safflower)

- 2 pinto beans, rinsed and cooked 1 cup of black beans

- 1 cup tomatoes with juice, chopped and unsalted, 1 cup sour cream, 3 big garlic cloves, minced or pressed (depending on preference)

- 1 tbsp. chickpea flour (optional) 1 teaspoon dried oregano 1 tablespoon of onion granules

- 1/2 teaspoon of salt

- 1/2 tsp. red chili flakes, finely chopped

- Spraying with cooking oil (sunflower, safflower, or refined coconut)

- For the crust, use the following ingredients:

- 1/2 cup yellow cornmeal, crushed to a fine powder

- 1 1/2 glasses of water are required.

- 1/2 teaspoon of salt

- 1 teaspoon of nutritional yeast

- 1 teaspoon of neutral-flavored olive oil (sunflower, safflower, or refined coconut)

- 2 tablespoons coarsely chopped cilantro

- 1/2 teaspoon lime zest

Directions:

- To prepare the filling, follow these steps:

- Toss the zucchini and oil together in a large pan set over medium-high heat for 3 minutes or until the zucchini begins to brown.

- In a large mixing bowl, combine the beans, tomatoes, garlic, flour, oregano, onion, salt, and chili flakes until well combined. Cook, often stirring, over medium heat for 5 minutes or until the mixture has thickened and there is no liquid remaining. Take the pan off the heat.

- Spray a 6-inch-round, 2-inch-deep baking pan with nonstick cooking spray and press the mixture into the bottom of the pan. Set the top aside when it has been smoothed out.

- To make the crust, follow these steps:

- Place the cornmeal, water, and salt in a medium-sized saucepan and boil over high heat. While bringing the mixture to a boil, continue to whisk continually. Once the water begins to boil, lower the heat to a very low setting. Pour in the Nutrition yeast and oil and simmer, constantly stirring, for 10 minutes or until the mixture is extremely thick and difficult to whisk. Then, take the pan off the heat.

- The cilantro and lime zest should be stirred into the cornmeal mixture until well mixed. Then, using a rubber spatula, carefully spread the mixture evenly over the contents in the baking pan to produce a smooth crust topping. Set aside. Pour everything into an air fryer basket and cook for 20 minutes until the top is golden brown. Allow it to cool for 5 to 10 minutes before cutting and serving.

Nutrition:

- Calories: 165 Total fat: 5g Saturated fat: 0 Calories

- 1 gram of fat Cholesterol: 0 milligrams Sodium: 831 milligrams 26 g of carbohydrates Fiber:6g

- 6 g of protein

Buffalo Cauliflower Bites

Time required for preparation: 25 minutes 4 portions (servings)

Ingredients:

- 1 head of cauliflower

- three garlic cloves

- a cup and a half Oil from extra-virgin olives

- Salt Pepper

- To make the sauce, combine the following ingredients:

- Hot sauce is a type of condiment. Butter Worcestershire sauce is a sauce made with butter and Worcestershire sauce.

Directions:

- Cut the cauliflower into florets of the same size and set them in a large mixing basin.

- Cut each garlic clove into three pieces and crush them with the side of your knife to release the flavor. Don't be frightened to squish the garlic cloves together. For the garlic to cook properly, you want to expose as much of its surface as possible. Add this to the cauliflower and mix well.

• Pour the oil over the top and season with salt. Using your hands, massage the cauliflower until it is thoroughly coated with the oil and salt.

• Set the air fryer at 400 degrees Fahrenheit for 20 minutes, and add the cauliflower. Turn it into a half-ounce measure.

• To prepare the sauce, follow these steps:

• Make the sauce while the cauliflower is roasting in the oven. Whisk together the spicy sauce, butter, and Worcestershire sauce in a small mixing bowl.

• Once the cauliflower has been cooked, transfer it to a large mixing basin. Pour the spicy sauce over the cauliflower and toss everything together.

- Place the cauliflower in the air fryer one more. Preheat the oven to 400 degrees Fahrenheit for 3-4 minutes or until the sauce is somewhat stiff.

- Toss with blue cheese dressing before serving.

Nutrition:

69 calories per serving

1.87 grams of protein

6.06 g of fat

carbohydrate (g): 1.99 g carbohydrate

Steak Bites with Mushrooms cooked in the air fryer.

Time required for preparation: 25 minutes 4 portions (servings)

Ingredients:

- Steaks weighing 1 pound, sliced into 1/2-inch chunks (rib eye, sirloin, tri-tip), 8 ounces of mushrooms

- Oil from extra-virgin olives 1 tablespoon of chili polder

- 1 teaspoon dried oregano

- 1/2 teaspoons garlic powder

- 1/4 tsp. Cayenne pepper Kosher salt is a kind of salt that is kosher.

- Peppercorns that have been freshly ground Coriander 2 red pepper flakes, chopped dill

Directions:

- Preheat the empty air fryer to 390°F for 4 minutes, using a crisp plate or basket to help with the heat distribution.

- Remove the meat from the pan and pat it dry. As the air fryer is heating up, toss the meat cubes with olive oil and Montreal seasonings to cook until done.

- Slice mushrooms in half or half again. Pour the meat cubes and mushrooms into the hot air fryer and gently shake the mixture to blend it all.

- Set the temperature of the air fryer to 390 degrees Fahrenheit and the timer for 8 minutes.

- After 3 minutes, come to a halt and shake the basket. Cook the beef cubes in batches of 2 minutes at a time until they achieve the desired degree of doneness. Lift a large piece of meat out and test it with a meat thermometer, or split a large piece of meat in half and look in the center to see how it's progressing. It is important to note that the meat will continue to cook even after it has been withdrawn from the air fryer and allowed to rest. The meat is medium-rare when it reaches 1/45°F and has a warm pink core.

- Toss the pork with the vegetables and set it aside for a few minutes before serving.

Nutrition:

- Calories in a serving: 583

- Protein content: 32.38 g

- 27.25 g of fat

- There are 61.98 grams of carbohydrates in total.

Pecan Crusted Chicken.

Time required for preparation: 25 minutes Ingredients: 6 servings Servings: 6

- 6 pieces of chicken tenders salt that is kosher

- paprika, freshly ground black pepper and cayenne pepper

- 2 tablespoons of honey

- 1 tablespoon of toasted mustard pecans

Directions:

- In a large mixing basin, combine the chicken tenders.

- Season the chicken with salt, pepper, and smoked paprika, and toss well until the chicken is evenly coated with the spices.

- Combine the honey and mustard in a large mixing bowl.

- Place the pecans on a platter and gently chop them up.

- Roll the chicken tenders in the shredded pecans, one at a time, until both sides are completely coated with the nuts. Excess material should be brushed away.

- Place the coated offers in the air fryer basket and repeat the process until all of the offers have been coated and are in the air fryer basket (around 20 minutes).

- Before serving, heat the chicken in the air fryer at 350°F for 1/2 minutes, until the chicken is cooked and the nuts are golden brown.

Nutrition:

- 95 calories per serving
- 3.08 grams of protein
- 8.18 g of fat
- Carbohydrates (in grams): 3.16 grams

Chicken Tikka Kebab

Time required for preparation: 30 minutes 6 individual servings

- Boneless and skinless chicken thighs are available. Onion (red)

- Green and red bell peppers are used in this recipe.

- For the marinade, combine the following ingredients:

- Yogurt Ginger Garlic Spices from India

Directions:

- In a large mixing basin, combine all the marinade ingredients and thoroughly mix them. Place the chicken in a large mixing bowl and distribute the marinade over both sides. Allow it to rest in the refrigerator from 30 minutes to 8 hours.

- Cook the marinated vegetables by adding oil, onions, and green and red peppers to the marinade. Make a thorough mix.

- In between the skewers, thread the marinated chicken, peppers, and onions onto the skewers.

- Lightly oil the air fryer basket with cooking spray.

- Prepare the chicken sticks in the Air fryer by arranging them in a single layer. Cook them for 10 minutes at 180 degrees Celsius.

- Cook the chicken sticks for another 7 minutes on the other side before serving.

Nutrition:

- Calories in a serving: 1/47

- Protein content: 10.25 g

- 10.68 g of fat

- carbohydrate: 1.85 g carbohydrate

Brussels Sprouts Cooked in the Air Fryer

Preparation time: 15 minutes Ingredients: Ingredients: Servings: 2

- 1/4 cup balsamic vinegar roasted Brussels sprouts

- extra-virgin olive oil (around 3 tablespoons) Kosher salt is a kind of salt that is kosher.

- peppercorns that have been freshly ground

Directions:

- Preparation: Remove the tough ends of the Brussels sprouts and any damaged outer leaves from the Brussels sprouts before cooking. Rinse thoroughly with cold water and pat dry. If your sprouts are huge, you may want to chop them in half. Combine the oil, salt, and pepper in a mixing bowl.

- Using your air fryer, arrange the Brussels sprouts in a single layer and cook in batches if they don't fit all in at once. Cook for 8 to 1/2 minutes at 190°C, shaking the pan halfway during the cooking time to ensure that the meat is uniformly browned. When they are gently browned and crispy around the edges, they are ready to serve.

- Serving suggestions: Warm sprouts can be served with balsamic reduction and parmesan if desired.

Nutrition:

- Calories:119 Protein content: 1/25.58 g

- 65.97 g of total fat

- Sugars and carbohydrates: 16.97 g

Crispy Tofu Cooked in the Air.

Preparation time: 50 minutes. There are 8 servings in total.

Ingredients:

- 2 blocks of extra-firm tofu (16 ounces) (453 g) 2 tablespoons soy sauce (30 ml)

- 1 tablespoon toasted sesame oil

- 1 tbsp. Olive oil

- 1 minced garlic clove (about)

Directions:

- Squeeze: Using either a heavy pan or a pan on top, squeeze the tofu for at least 15 minutes to allow the liquid to drain away. When you're finished, chop the tofu into bite-sized blocks and place it in a large mixing bowl.

- Taste: In a small mixing bowl, combine the remaining ingredients. Drizzle the dressing over the tofu and toss to coat. Allow the tofu to marinade for an additional 15 minutes.

- Air fryer (also known as a deep fryer): Preheat your air fryer to 190 degrees Celsius. Toss the tofu blocks into the air fryer basket in a single layer and set aside. Allow 10 to 15 minutes of cooking time, and shake the pan regularly to ensure equal cooking throughout.

Nutrition:

- Calories in a serving: 247

- 3.83 g of protein, 18.05 g of fat

- g of carbohydrates (21.99 g)

Crispy Baked Avocado Tacos.

Preparation time: 20 minutes Ingredients: 5 servings (serves 5)

- 1 cup pineapple, coarsely chopped for the salsa

- 1 Roma tomato, peeled and cut finely

- 1/2 ounce of coarsely sliced red bell pepper

- 1/2 of a medium red onion (about) 1 garlic clove, peeled and minced

- 1/2 jalapeño peppers, finely diced, a pinch of cumin, and a pinch of salt

- Tacos with avocado:

- 1 avocado (per person)

- 1/4 cup unbleached all-purpose flour 35 g (grams) 1 large egg, lightly whisked

- 1/2 cup panko bread crumbs 65 g (grams) Using a pinch of salt and pepper, season the dish.

- 4 tortillas de harina (flour tortillas). Recipes may be found by clicking here.

- 1/4 cup plain yogurt for the adobo sauce (60 g) 2 tablespoons of mayonnaise (30 g)

- 1/4 teaspoon lime juice

- 1 tablespoon chipotle pepper adobo sauce from a jar of chipotle peppers Polte peppers is a kind of pepper.

Directions:

- Preparing the salsa: Combine the ingredients and place them in the refrigerator.

- Prepare the avocado by halving it lengthwise and removing the pit from the center. Next, place the avocado peel facing down on a cutting board and chop each half into four equal halves. After that, gently peel away the skin.

- Station for preparation: Preheat the oven to 230 degrees Celsius (440 degrees Fahrenheit) or the air fryer to 190 degrees Celsius (374 degrees Fahrenheit). Set up your work space so that you have a bowl of flour, a bowl of a whisk, a bowl of Panko with salt and pepper, and a baking sheet coated with parchment paper at the end of the table.

- Finish by dipping each avocado slice in flour, then in the egg, and last in the panko. Place on the baking sheet that has been prepared and bake for 10 minutes, or fry in the air. After about half of the cooking time, the potatoes are lightly browned.

- Sauce: Mix the sauce ingredients in a small bowl while the avocados are cooking.

- To assemble, spread salsa on a tortilla, top with 2 slices of avocado, then drizzle with sauce. Serve quickly and have pleasure in it!

Nutritional Information:

- 193 calories

- Protein content: 13.7 g

- 13.25 g of fat

- Carbohydrates (in grams): 4.69 g

Cod in butter sauce.

Preparation time: 15 minutes 4 portions (servings)

Ingredients:

- 1 tablespoon finely chopped parsley 3 tablespoons melted butter 8 cherry tomatoes, halved 0.25 cup tomato sauce 2 fish fillets, cut into cubes

Directions:

- Preheat the air fryer to 390 degrees Fahrenheit.

- Combine all the ingredients in a pan compatible with an air fryer and bake for 30 minutes.

- After 1/2 minutes of baking, you may divide the mixture among the four serving dishes and serve immediately.

Nutrition:

- Calories in a serving: 232 Carbohydrates: 5 g 11 g of protein 8 g of fat

Chicken in cream sauce.

Preparation time: 20 minutes 4 portions (servings)

Ingredients:

- 1 teaspoon of pepper and salt
- 1/2 teaspoon of extra-virgin olive oil
- Paprika with a sweet taste
- 0.25 cup cream cheese (optional)
- 4 chicken breasts cut into cubes

Directions:

- Preheat the air fryer to 370 degrees Fahrenheit.

- Prepare a pan that will fit into the machine by rubbing it with a little oil before adding the ingredients.

- Place this in the air fryer and bake for a few minutes. Then, after 17 minutes, divide the mixture among the few dishes and serve it!

Nutrition:

- 250 calories Carbohydrates: 5 g 11 g of protein 1/2 g of fat

Stew with mushrooms and turkey.

Time required for preparation: 25 minutes 4 portions (servings)

Ingredients:

- A pinch of pepper and a pinch of salt

- 1/4 cup tomato sauce 1 tablespoon parsley, finely chopped 0.25 cup tomato sauce brown mushrooms, sliced 1 turkey breast (cubed) 1 turkey breast (cut into cubes)

Directions:

- Preheat the air fryer to 350 degrees Fahrenheit.

- Remove the turkey from the oven and place it in a skillet with the tomato sauce, pepper, salt, and mushrooms. Add the ingredients to the air fryer.

- After 25 minutes, the stew is finished; divide it among four serving dishes and garnish it with parsley to serve.

Nutrition:

- 220 calories, 5 grams of carbohydrates, 1/2 g of fat, 1/2 g of protein

Chicken with basil sauce.

Time required for preparation: 25 minutes 4 portions (servings)

Ingredients:

- a pinch of pepper and a pinch of salt
- 2 teaspoons smoked paprika,
- 1/2 teaspoon dried basil
- 0.5 cup chicken stock (optional)
- diced chicken breasts weighing 0.5 pound

Directions:

- Preheat the air fryer to 390 degrees Fahrenheit.

- Bring out a pan and throw all ingredients into it before placing it in the air fryer to finish cooking.

- After 25 minutes in the oven, divide the mixture among a few dishes and serve with a side salad.

Nutrition:

- Calories in 1 serving: 223 Carbohydrates: 5 g 13 g of protein 1/2 g of fat

Baked Eggplant.

Preparation time: 15 minutes 4 portions (servings)

Ingredients:

- 2 tbsp. Olive oil, freshly ground pepper, and salt
- 6 green spring onions (chopped),
- 1 hot chili pepper (chopped),
- 2 eggplants (cubed),
- 4 garlic cloves (minced),
- 1/2 cup cilantro (chopped),
- 1/2 pound cherry tomatoes (cubed).

Directions:

- Turn on the air fryer and let it heat up to 380 degrees Fahrenheit.
- Bake the ingredients in a baking pan that will be placed in the air fryer once they have been mixed.

- Place the ingredients into the air fryer to cook. After 15 minutes, divide the mixture among four serving dishes and serve immediately.

Nutrition:

- Calories in a serving: 232 Carbohydrates: 5 g 1/2 g of fat 10 g of protein

Meatball Casserole

Preparation time: 15 minutes, 6 individual servings

Ingredients:

- 1/4 cup parsley, chopped
- 1/4 cup fresh thyme
- 1/3 pound turkey sausage
- 1 tablespoon fresh thyme

- 1 egg, lightly beaten

- 1/3 pound. cooked ground beef

- 2 tablespoons extra-virgin olive oil

- 1 tbsp. Dijon mustard

- 1 shallot, finely chopped 3 garlic cloves, minced 2 tbsp. skimmed milk 3 tablespoons olive oil

- 1 tbsp. Finely chopped rosemary

Directions:

- Set the air fryer to the High setting and let it heat up for a few minutes with a small amount of oil inside.

- Cook for a few minutes to soften the garlic and onions before adding the rest of the ingredients.

- Mix the milk and bread crumbs in a large mixing dish. Then combine all of the remaining ingredients and lay them aside to soak.

- After five minutes, use this mixture to make some little meatballs by rolling them in breadcrumbs. Place them in the air fryer and cook until crispy.

- To cook, raise the temperature to 400 degrees Fahrenheit. After 10 minutes, remove the cover from the basket and shake it vigorously. Cook for a further five minutes before removing from the heat.

Nutrition:

- Calories in a serving: 168

- Carbohydrates: 4 g

- 1/2 g of protein

- 11 g of fat

Baked Beef.

Preparation time: 1-hour Ingredients: 3 servings of each type

- 1 bunch of garlic cloves (about)

- 1 bunch of fresh herbs, preferably mixed 2 onions, thinly sliced Extra virgin olive oil 3 lbs. beef celery sticks, chopped 2 carrots, chopped 3 lbs. beef celery sticks, chopped

Directions:

- Prepare a pan by heating it on the stovetop and then add the herbs, olive oil, beef roast, and veggies.

- Preheat the air fryer to 400 degrees Fahrenheit and set the pan inside. Allow this to boil, and then cover it with a lid.

- After an hour of cooking, remove the lid and serve the dish immediately, if possible.

Nutrition:

- Calories in a serving: 306 Carbohydrates: 10g 21 g of fat 32 g of protein

Pillows made of turkey.

Preparation time: 15 minutes 4 portions (servings)

Ingredients:

- 15 slices of smoked turkey breast

- 2 jars of cream cheese (optional)

- 1 egg yolk (optional)

- 4 cups of all-purpose flour

- Halfa tablespoon of granulated yeast, preferably dry, 2 tablespoons of sugar

- 3/4 teaspoon of salt

- 1/3 cup extra-virgin olive oil

- 1/3 cup of distilled water

- 1 cup milk with an egg yolk in it.

Directions:

- Using your hands, combine the ingredients for the dough until they are smooth. Make little balls out of it and place them on a floured surface.

- To make the dough balls square, open them up with a rolling pin. Cut the chicken into tiny pieces. Fill the cavity with turkey breast and a small amount of cream cheese. Bring all of the points together.

- Preheat the air fryer to 400 degrees Fahrenheit. Place a handful of the balls inside and allow them to cook for a few minutes.

- Take them out after five minutes and repeat the process with the remainder of the pillows until you're through.

Nutrition:

- Calories in a serving: 528 Carbohydrates: 23 g 30 g of fat 44 g of protein

Chicken wings

Time required for preparation: 25 minutes
Ingredients: Ingredients: Servings: 2

- 2 tbsp. chopped chives

- 0.5 teaspoon of salt 1 tablespoon of lime juice

- 0.5 tablespoons grated ginger, finely chopped 1 tablespoon minced garlic

- 1 tablespoon of chili paste

- 1 tablespoon of honey

- 0.5 tablespoon of cornstarch

- 1 tablespoon of soy sauce Oil

- 10 pieces of chicken wings

Directions:

- Spray the chicken with cooking spray once it has been dried. Place the ingredients in an air fryer that has been preheated to 400oF.

- Allow this to simmer for a few minutes. During this time, combine the other ingredients in a large mixing basin and put it aside.

- The chicken is done after 25 minutes in the oven. Place the chicken in a bowl and drizzle the sauce on top. Serve with a sprinkle of chives on top if desired.

Nutrition:

- Calories in a serving: 81 Carbohydrates: 0g 5 g of fat 8 g of protein

Chapter Five

Dinner

Honey-Lime Chicken Wings

Time required for preparation: 30 minutes 4 portions (servings)

Ingredients:

- 2 pounds. boneless chicken wings with lime juice (about 2 tablespoons)

- 0.25 cup molasses 1 tablespoon of lime zest

- a garlic clove that has been squeezed

Directions:

- Heat the Air Fryer to 360 degrees Fahrenheit.

- Combine the garlic, honey, lime juice, and zest in a mixing bowl. In a large mixing bowl, combine the wings and the sauce.

- Prepare the wings in batches to save time. Cook for 25-30 minutes or until the potatoes are crisp and golden. Shake the basket every 8 minutes throughout the first 8 minutes.

- Garnish with fresh herbs if desired.

Nutrition:

- Calories in this recipe: 375

- Protein content: 51.59 g

- 9.56 g of fat

- Carbohydrates (in grams): 18.67 g

Whole chicken cooked in a rotisserie.

Time required for preparation: 30 minutes 4 portions (servings)

Ingredients:

- 2 tablespoons of extra-virgin olive oil, as needed, 6-7 pound entire chicken (serves 4-6 people)

- 1 tbsp. Salt, seasoning to taste

Directions:

- Preheat the Air Fryer to 350 degrees Fahrenheit.

- Season the chicken breasts with a drizzle of oil and a pinch of salt.

- Place the chicken in the Air Fryer skin-side and cook for 15 minutes.

- Cook for 30 minutes at low heat. Turn the chicken over and cook for another 30 minutes in the air fryer.

- Wait 10 minutes before chopping the meat.

- Note: This recipe is for birds weighing less than 6 lbs. and is designed to be cooked in a 3.7-quart Air Fryer.

Nutrition:

- Calories in 1 serving: 859

- Protein content: 151.45 g

- 23.67 g of total fat

- Carbohydrates (g): nil

Chicken with Tarragon.

Preparation time: 1/2 minute 1 serving (about).

Ingredients:

- 1 skinless/boneless chicken breast (serves 4)

- 0.1/25 tsp. freshly cracked black pepper (ground black pepper)

- 0.5 tablespoon unsalted butter and 0.1/25 teaspoon kosher salt

- 0.25 cup dried tarragon, minced

- In addition, the following is required: Aluminum foil is a kind of aluminum foil (1/2x1/4-inch piece)

Directions:

- Pre-heat the oven to 390 degrees Fahrenheit in advance.

- Arrange the chicken in a single layer on aluminum foil with the tarragon, butter, salt, and pepper.

- Wrap the foil loosely to allow for the least amount of airflow.

- In an air fryer basket, cook the chicken packets for 1/2 minutes at 350°F.

Nutrition:

- Calories in a serving: 101

- 6.53 grams of protein

- 8.02 g of fat

- Carbohydrates: 0.53 g (total carbohydrate content).

Chicken Breast with Lemon Juice.

Time required for preparation: 30 minutes 4 portions (servings)

Ingredients:

- 1/4 cup extra-virgin olive oil

- 3 tablespoons minced garlic

- 1 cup dry white wine (about)

- 1 tablespoon freshly grated lemon zest 2 tbsp. freshly squeezed lemon juice

- dried oregano leaves (crushed) between 1 and 1/2tsp 1 tablespoon chopped thyme leaves

- season with salt and pepper to taste

- 4 chicken breasts, skin-on, boneless and skinless, 1 lemon, thinly sliced

Directions:

- Take a baking dish and toss in all specified ingredients before adding the chicken breasts and coating them thoroughly.

- Place lemon slices on top of the dish.

- Make an even layer of the mustard mixture on the toasted bread slices.

- Select "Air Fry" mode on your Air Fryer by pressing the "Power Button" on the appliance.

- To set the time, press the Time Button and select 30 minutes.

- Set the temperature to 370oF by pressing the Temp Button.

- Start the device by pressing the "Start/Pause" button on the remote control.

- Place the pan in the Air Fryer's Cooking basket and heat until the pan is completely cooked.

- Prepare the dish and serve it.

Nutrition:

- calorie count: 388

- 8 g total fat, 1 g saturated fat

- 8 grams of carbohydrates

- 1 gram of dietary fiber

- Sodium content: 339 mg Protein content: 13 g

Lemon and Chicken Pepper.

Preparation time: 15 minutes 4 portions (servings)

Ingredients:

- 1 pound of chicken breasts

- 1 lemon, juiced with the rind set aside

- 1 tablespoon poultry seasoning

- 1 teaspoon of garlic purée a little handful of peppercorns

- season with salt and pepper to taste

Directions:

- Preheat your fryer to 352 degrees Fahrenheit in the setting.

- Take a big piece of silver foil and, working from the top down, sprinkle all of the spices and lemon peel on top of it.

- Prepare the chicken breast by laying it on a cutting board and trimming away any excess fat and small bones.

- Season both sides of the chicken with pepper and salt.

- Both sides of the chicken should be well-seasoned with the seasoning.

- Place your silver foil sheet on top of it and massage it in.

- It should be properly sealed.

- Roll it out flat with a rolling pin to make it more manageable.

- Place it in your fryer for 15 minutes or until the center is completely cooked through.

Nutrition: Simply prepare and serve.

- Calories in a serving: 350

- Saturated fatty acids: 33 g

- 9 g of fat

- There are 2 grams of carbohydrates in this recipe.

- 0 g of dietary fiber

- Sodium content: 330 mg Protein content: 33 g

Edamame and asparagus served with chicken curry.

Preparation time: 10 minutes Ingredients: 4 servings (servings per recipe)

- 1 teaspoon cumin, freshly ground

- a 1/2oz boneless and skinless chicken breast, 2 quarts of water

- 1/4 tsp. freshly ground black pepper

- 1/4 cup light mayonnaise (optional)

- 1 cup plain Greek yogurt (1/4 cup total) 1 to 1/2 teaspoons curry powder

- 1/2 teaspoon of salt

- 1 tablespoon of sugar

- 2 cups of asparagus, sliced

- 4 cups baby kale mix (optional)

- 3 cups cooked, shelled edamame, thawed 1 cup edamame

- 1/4 cup finely chopped green onion or cilantro

- 1/2 cup finely chopped red onion

Directions:

- Season the chicken with pepper and cumin and cook it for 6 minutes in the air fryer. Allow the pressure to naturally release before removing the cover and the chicken.

- Keep it on the cutting board for 5 minutes, then shred and set it away.

- In a mixing basin, whisk together the mayonnaise, yogurt, salt, curd, and sugar until well combined.

- Cook the edamame and asparagus for 1 minute after adding them to the saucepan.

- Release the pressure and retain the asparagus mixture in the colander. *** Run this under cold water and let it drain completely.

- Place equal amounts of the kale mixture on each of the four dishes. Then, on top of the asparagus combination, place the feta cheese.

- Toss the onions and chicken with the yogurt mixture until everything is completely coated.

- Distribute equal amounts of the asparagus mixture on each serving plate and garnish with cilantro.

Nutrition:

- Calories in a serving: 253 17 g of carbohydrates Total fat (g): 9 g 26 g of protein Fiber:5g

Rib Eye Steak

Preparation time: 35 minutes 2 portions (servings)

Ingredients:

- 2 lb. steak, uncooked and unchilled

- 1 tablespoon of extra-virgin olive oil

- Steak rub: season with salt and pepper to taste A baking pan was also required to fit within the basket.

Directions:

- To access the French Fries icon, use the "M" button on your keyboard. Set the timer for four minutes at 400 degrees Fahrenheit.

- Season the steak with the oil and spices before grilling it. Place the steak in the basket and cook for 1/4 minute in the air fryer. It should be turned in after seven minutes.)

- Place the rib eye on a dish and let it aside for 10 minutes to rest before carving.

- It may be sliced and garnished in any way you wish.

Nutrition:

- Calories:350 Protein content: 1/29.44 g
- 55.78 g of total fat
- Carbohydrates (g): nil

Chicken Wings Cooked in the Air Fryer

Preparation time: 20 minutes 4 portions (servings)

Ingredients:

- 1 pound of chicken wings 1 tablespoon of grainy mustard 1 clove of garlic minced garlic (finely chopped)
- 1 tablespoon finely minced shallots
- 2 tablespoons finely chopped fresh thyme, plus more for garnish 2 tbsp. Finely chopped fresh rosemary

- , kosher salt, and the juice of a one-twelfth lemon

- peppercorns that have been freshly ground. Lemon slices, to be used as a garnish

Directions:

- Removing the chicken wing portions from the refrigerator and patting them dry is the first step (if you remove as much moisture as possible, you will get a crispy wing skin).

- In a small bowl or baking dish, combine the sea salt, black pepper, smoked paprika, garlic powder, onion powder, and baking powder until well combined.

- Sprinkle the spice mixture on the wings and cover them with aluminum foil.

- Placing the wings in the frying basket is a good idea. This is called the "Cook & Crisp" basket in the Ninja Foodie game.

- Olive oil should be drizzled over the chicken wings.

- Cook the wings for 1/4 minute on each side at 400 degrees Fahrenheit using the Air Crisp setting on air fryers.

- Enjoy some sizzling wings!

Nutrition:

- Calories in a serving: 32

- 2 g of protein

- 1.73 g of fat

- Carbohydrates (in grams): 2.56 grams

Montreal Steak in a sweet and spicy sauce.

Preparation time: 6 minutes Ingredients: Ingredients: Servings: 2

- boneless sirloin steaks (serves 2)

- 1 tablespoon of brown sugar

- 1 tbsp. of the mixture Seasoning for steaks in Montreal

- 1 tbsp. Red pepper smashed 1 tbsp. thyme, chopped

- Olive oil is a kind of oil that comes from the olive tree.

Directions:

- The temperature of the Air Fryer should be set to 390oF.

- Prepare the steaks by brushing them with oil. Season them by rubbing them with the seasonings of your choice.

- Place the steaks in a basket and set a timer for 3 minutes to cook them through.

- Turn the steak over and cook for another 3 minutes in the air fryer.

- Before serving, allow it to cool and then slice it into strips.

Nutrition:

- calorie count: 1/253

- Protein content: 1/26.25 g

- 75.9 g of fat

- Carbohydrates (in grams): 6.58 grams

Scallops with Dill, steamed in a steamer.

Preparation time: 4 minutes 4 portions (servings)

Ingredients:

- 1 pound of sea scallops

- 1 tablespoon freshly squeezed lemon juice
2 tablespoons extra-virgin olive oil

- 1 teaspoon dried dill and a pinch of salt

- peppercorns that have been freshly ground

Directions:

- Check the scallops for a little muscle connected to the side, and if you find one, rip it out and throw it away.

- Toss the scallops with the lemon juice, olive oil, dill, salt, and pepper in a large mixing bowl until well coated. Place the ingredients in the air fryer basket.

• Scallops should be firm when checked with a finger after 4 to 5 minutes of steaming (with the basket tossed once throughout cooking time). At a bare minimum, the interior temperature should be 1/45°F.

Nutrition:

• Total fat: 3g Saturated fat: 0g Calories: 1/21 Total fat: 3g 37 milligrams of cholesterol Sodium: 223 milligrams 3 g of carbohydrates Fiber:0g

• 19 g of protein

Chicken Cacciatore.

Preparation time: 15 minutes 4 portions (servings)

Ingredients:

- 4 thighs of chicken
- 2 tablespoons extra-virgin olive oil
- 4 oz. mushrooms, sliced
- 2 cloves garlic, minced 2 tbsp.
- Tomato paste 1/2 onion, minced
- 3 celery stalks, minced
- 2 tbsp. tomato paste
- 1/4 oz. tomatoes, stewed and in a tomato sauce 2 teaspoons of Provence herbs
- 1/4 cup water 3 cubes chicken bouillon, crushed 3 cubes chicken stock season with pepper to taste
- Add a pinch of red pepper flakes.

Directions:

- Set the sauté function on your Instant Pot.

- Cook the chicken for 5 to 6 minutes per side in the oil once it has been added.

- Place on a serving dish.

- Toss onion, celery, and mushrooms to the saucepan and mix well.

- Cook for 5 minutes on medium heat.

- Cook for 2 minutes once you've added the garlic.

- Bring the chicken back to the pot.

- Combine the tomato paste, herbs, bouillon, and water in a large mixing bowl.

- Put the lid on the saucepan.

- Cook for 1/2 minutes on high heat.

- Release the pressure as soon as possible.

- Before serving, sprinkle the pepper and red flakes on top of the dish.

Nutrition:

- Calories in 1 serving: 392.4

- Saturated fat: 5.8 g Total fat: 24.5 g

- Carbohydrates (in grams): 13.6 g

- 2.7 g of dietary fiber

- Protein content: 29.9 g

- 96.1 milligrams of cholesterol

- 7.3 g of sugars Sodium: 1072.6 milligrams Potassium content: 71/4.8 milligrams

Chicken with Salsa.

Preparation time: 15 minutes Ingredients: Ingredients: Servings: 2

- 1 pound boneless skinless chicken breast fillet taco seasoning mix (one ounce)

- 1/2 cup of salsa

- 1/2 cup chicken broth (preferably low-sodium)

Directions:

- Taco seasoning mix should be used to season the chicken breast fillet.

- Place the chicken in the Instant Pot and seal the lid. On top, spread the salsa evenly.

- Add the chicken broth and mix well.

- Keep the cover firmly in place.

- Select the poultry setting from the drop-down menu. Set the timer for 15 minutes. Pressure may be released naturally.

- With a fork, shred the chicken breasts.

Nutrition:

- Nutritional Values: 300.1 calories

- Fat: 4.8 g Saturated Fatty Acids

- 1.4 g of fat

- Carbohydrates (in grams): 13.9 g

- 1 gram of dietary fiber

- Protein content: 45.9 g

- 118 milligrams of cholesterol

- 4.6 g of sugars

- Sodium: 1045.5 milligrams

- Potassium content: 476.5 milligrams

Curry with chicken.

Time required for preparation: 25 minutes

4 portions (servings)

Ingredients:

- 1 tablespoon of coconut oil 1 medium onion, minced

- crushed and chopped 2 cloves garlic, to taste curry powder (about 3 tablespoons)

- 2 tablespoons granulated sugar

- 8 ounces of tomato sauce (from a can)

- 1/4 oz. tomatoes, diced and from a can

- 1/2 cup chicken broth (about)

- 2 lbs. boneless skinless chicken breast fillet season with salt and pepper to taste 1/4 ounces of skimmed milk

Directions:

- The sauté function on your Instant Pot should be selected.

- Pour in the coconut oil until it is completely absorbed.

- Cook the onion and garlic for 2 minutes or until they are translucent.

- Stir in the curry powder until it is evenly distributed.

- To cancel the action, press the "Cancel" button.

- Combine the sugar, tomato sauce, and chicken stock in a large mixing bowl. Stir.

- Season both sides of the chicken breasts with salt and pepper before grilling.

- Place the chicken in the pot and cover it with water.

- Put the pot in a safe place.

- Cook for 10 minutes on high heat.

- Pressure may be released naturally.

- Return the chicken to the pot when it has been shredded.

- Select the sauté option.

- Cook for 3 minutes on medium heat.

- Pour in the skimmed milk and stir well.

- Cook for a further 10 minutes.

Nutrition:

- Fat: 30.6 g Saturated fat: 23.1 g Calories: 563.3 Fat: 30.6 g

- 21.5 grams of carbohydrates

- 4.9 g of dietary fiber

- Protein content: 51.9 g

- 1/2.5 grams of sugar

- Cholesterol level: 130 milligrams

- Sodium: 766.2 milligrams

- Potassium is 1038.3 milligrams per kilogram of body weight.

Stew with beef.

Preparation time: 40 minutes

4 portions (servings)

Ingredients:

- 1 tbsp. melted butter

- 1 pound chuck roast, cut into cubes 1 onion, quartered; 2 garlic cloves, smashed and chopped; 1 tablespoon olive oil 1/2-cups mushrooms, halved or split in half 4 potatoes, peeled and cut into cubes

- carrots, peeled and sliced

- 2 cups beef broth (preferably low-sodium)

- Worcestershire sauce

- 1 tablespoon of tomato paste season with salt and pepper to taste

- 1/2 tbsp. rosemary, preferably dried

Directions:

- The sauté function on your Instant Pot should be selected.

- Cook the meat for 5 minutes in the butter after adding it.

- Combine the onion, garlic, mushrooms, potatoes, and carrots in a large mixing bowl.

- Keep the cover firmly in place.

- To use the meat/stew feature, press the button.

- Set the timer for 35 minutes.

- Pressure may be released naturally.

- Bowls should be used for serving.

Nutrition:

- Calories: 351.7 Fat: 16.4 g Saturated Fat: 7.2 g Total Calories: 351.7
- 33.22 g of carbohydrate calories
- 4 g of dietary fiber
- 20 g of protein
- 59.1 milligrams of cholesterol
- 4.6 g of sugars
- Sodium: 1020.5 milligrams
- Potassium is 541.8 milligrams.

Pot Roast with Veggies

Approximately 1 hour and 10 minutes of cooking time. There are 8 servings in total.

Ingredients:

- 4 tablespoons extra-virgin olive oil, split
- 3-pound chuck roast of beef
- 2 cups beef broth with a reduced salt content
- 1 onion, peeled and cut into wedges
- 1 package dry onion soup mix (optional). 1 1/2 cups baby carrots (optional)
- 1 pound of baby potatoes
- 1/2 tablespoons cornstarch dissolved in 1/4 cup water season with pepper to taste
- 1 and a half teaspoons of garlic salt

Directions:

- In your Instant Pot, choose the sauté function.

- Half of the oil should be added to the saucepan.

- Cook the chuck roast for 4 minutes per side or until it is done.

- Pour the broth into the pot.

- Combine the oil, onion, soup mix, carrots, and potatoes in a large mixing dish.

- Fill the saucepan halfway with the mixture.

- Put the lid on the saucepan.

- Cook for 1 hour on high heat.

- Release the pressure as soon as possible.

- Placing the roast on a serving platter.

- Select the sauté option.

- Fill the saucepan halfway with the cornstarch mixture.

- Cook for 3 minutes on medium heat.

- Pepper and garlic salt are added to the sauce to season it.

- Serve the roast with vegetables and sauce on the side.

Nutrition:

- Calories consumed: 323.2

- Fat: 15.6 g, of which 15.6 g is saturated

- 4.4 g of fat

- Carbohydrates (in grams): 19 g

- 2.6 g of dietary fiber

- Protein content: 25.7 g

- Cholesterol: 788 milligrams

- 2.4 g of sugars

- Sodium: 1005.4 milligrams

- Potassium content: 587.2 milligrams

Mexican Rice.

Preparation time: 20 minutes Ingredients: 4 servings (servings per recipe)

- 1 tablespoon of avocado oil

- 1 / 2 onion, finely chopped

- crushed and chopped 2 cloves garlic, to taste 1 cup cooked rice

- 1/2 cups chicken broth (preferably low-sodium)

- 1/2 cup tomato sauce (low-sodium version) 1/2 teaspoon cayenne pepper

- 1/4 tsp. cumin seeds, crushed season with salt to taste

Directions:

- To use the sauté feature in your Instant Pot, press the Sauté button.

- Pour the avocado oil into the saucepan and stir to combine.

- Cook the onion and garlic for 5 minutes, turning regularly until the onion is translucent.

- Add in the rice and mix well.

- Apply a thin layer of oil.

- Add the chicken stock and mix well.

- Add the cayenne pepper, cumin, and salt and mix well.

- Put the lid on the saucepan.

- Cook for 15 minutes on high heat.

- Release the pressure as soon as possible.

- Serve the rice once it has been stirred.

Nutrition:

- Calories in a serving: 224.6

- Protein content: 5.2 g

- Carbohydrates (411.1 g) :

- 1.4 g of dietary fiber

- 2.2 g of sugars

- 4.1 g Saturated Fatty Acids

- 0.7 g of fat

- 1.5 milligrams of cholesterol

- Potassium content: 185.8 milligrams

- Sodium: 787.7 milligrams

Hamburger Soup (also known as Hamburger Noodle Soup).

Time required for preparation: 30 minutes

Ingredients: 8 servings (serves 8)

- 1 onion, finely chopped, 1 1/2 poundsof ground beef

- 45 ounces beef consommé in a can 10 oz. tomato soup (from a can)

- 28 ounces of canned and chopped tomatoes 2 quarts of water

- diced 3 celery stalks 4 carrots 1/2 teaspoon dry thyme 3 cups water 3 cups chicken broth 4 tbsp. pearl barley (optional) 1 bay leaf (optional)

Directions:

- In your Instant Pot, choose the sauté function.

- Combine the onion and meat in a large mixing bowl.

- Prepare the dish for 10 minutes, stirring often.

- Add in the rest of the ingredients and mix well.

- Close and secure the lid.

- Select the soup option from the drop-down menu.

- Cook for 30 minutes at low heat.

- Pressure may be released naturally.

- Remove the bay leaf and place the dish on a serving tray.

Nutrition:

- 251.1 calories, 11.2 g fat, 11.2 g saturated fat

- 4.3 g of fat

- Carbohydrates (in grams): 17.8 g

- 3.4 g of dietary fiber

- 18.7 grams of protein

- 51.7 milligrams of cholesterol

- 7.7 g of sugars

- Sodium: 950.4 milligrams

- Potassium content: 660.6 milligrams

Roasted Brussels Sprouts

Preparation time: 10 minutes 4 portions (servings)

Ingredients:

- 2 tablespoons extra-virgin olive oil 1-inch-thick slices of onion 1-pound entire Brussels sprouts—cut in half seasoning with salt and pepper

- 1/2 cup vegetable broth (optional)

Directions:

- Set the sauté function on your Instant Pot.

- Pour the olive oil into the saucepan and stir well.

- Cook the onion for 2 minutes on medium heat.

- Add in the Brussels sprouts and mix well.

- Cook for 1 minute at a time.

- Season with salt and pepper to taste.

- Add the veggie broth to the saucepan and bring it to a boil.

- Close and secure the lid.

- Cook for 3 minutes on high heat.

- Release the pressure as soon as possible.

Nutrition:

- Calories in a serving: 135.6

- Saturated fat: 7.2 g Total fat:

- 1 gram of fat

- Carbohydrates (in grams): 16.3 grams

- 5.5 g of fiber, 4.6 g of protein

- Cholesterol: 0 milligrams

- 5.3 g of sugars

- Sodium: 669.8 milligrams

- Potassium (in milligrams): 527.9 mg

Chicken with sesame sauce.

Preparation time: 20-25 minutes 4 portions (servings)

Ingredients:

- Soy sauce is a type of condiment. Pepper, salt, and extra-virgin olive oil Breadcrumbs Egg

- 1 pound of chicken breast

Directions:

- Fillet the chicken with the sesame oil and soy sauce, then toss everything together in a large mixing basin. Allow about a half-hour of marinating time.

- First, whisk together the eggs and then slide the chicken through them.

- Place the ingredients on the grill of an air fryer set to 350 degrees Fahrenheit. Allow it to grill for a few minutes.

- After 20 minutes, remove the chicken from the oven and allow it to cool before serving.

Nutrition:

- Calories in this recipe: 375 Carbohydrates: 6g 18 g of fat 35 g of protein

Thyme Turkey Breast.

Preparation time: 40 minutes 4 portions (servings)

Ingredients:

- 2 pounds of turkey breast season with salt to taste

- Season with freshly ground black pepper to taste 2 cups shredded chicken 4 tablespoons butter, melted 3 garlic cloves, minced 1 tbsp. Thyme, chopped 1 teaspoon rosemary, chopped

Directions:

- In a large mixing bowl, combine the butter, salt, black pepper, garlic, thyme, and rosemary.

- Season the turkey breast thoroughly with this spice mixture before placing it in the Air Fryer basket.

- The "Air Fry" mode may be selected by turning the dial.

- Press the Time button once more, and this duration turns the dial to set the cooking time to forty minutes.

- By now, you should have the temperature set at 375 degrees Fahrenheit by pressing and rotating the Temp button.

- After the oven has been warmed, insert the Air fryer basket into the oven.

- Slice and serve immediately.

Nutrition:

- Calories in a serving: 334

- 4.7 g of fat

- Carbohydrates: 54.1 g

- 26.2 g of protein per kilogram of body weight

Drumsticks de Cochinita (chicken drumsticks).

Preparation time: 20 minutes. There are 8 servings in total.

Ingredients:

- 8 pieces of chicken drumsticks 2 tablespoons extra-virgin olive oil

- 1 teaspoon of salt

- 1 tsp. Freshly ground pepper

- Garlic powder (one teaspoon) 1 teaspoon of paprika

- 1/2 teaspoon cumin

Directions:

- In a large mixing bowl, combine the olive oil, salt, black pepper, garlic powder, paprika, and cumin.

- Apply a generous amount of this mixture to all of the drumsticks.

- Using an Air fryer basket, place these drumsticks in the oven.

- The "Air Fry" mode may be selected by turning the dial.

- Press the Time button once more, and this duration turns the dial to set the cooking time to twenty minutes.

- By now, you should have the temperature set at 375 degrees Fahrenheit by pressing and rotating the Temp button.

- After the oven has been warmed, insert the Air fryer basket into the oven.

- When the drumsticks are half-cooked, turn them over and continue cooking.

- Continue air frying for the remaining 10 minutes of the time limit.

- Warm the dish before serving.

Nutrition:

- Calories: 21/2 per serving

- 11.8 g of total fat

- Carbohydrates: 1/4.6 g

- Protein content: 17.3 g

Chicken Bake with a Blackened Flavor.

Preparation time: 18 minutes 4 portions (servings)

Ingredients:

- 4 boneless skinless chicken breasts 2 tablespoons extra-virgin olive oil
- Seasoning:
- 1 1/2 tbsp. granulated sugar, 1 teaspoon of paprika
- 1 teaspoon dried oregano
- 1/4 tsp. garlic powder (optional)
- 1/2 teaspoon of salt and pepper
- Garnish:\Parsley, chopped

Directions:

- In a large mixing bowl, combine the olive oil, brown sugar, paprika, oregano, garlic powder, salt, and black pepper.

- Place the chicken breasts on a baking pan in the Ninja Oven and bake for 20 minutes.

- Pour and massage this mixture all over the chicken breasts until they are well coated.

- Selecting the "Bake" mode is accomplished by turning the dial.

- Press the Time button for a second duration and turn the dial to set the cooking time to 18 minutes this time.

- Now press the Temp button and turn the dial to 425 degrees Fahrenheit to complete the temperature setting process.

- Place the baking pan inside the oven after it has been warmed.

- Warm the dish before serving.

Nutrition:

- Calories in a serving: 41/2
- 24.8 g of total fat
- Carbohydrates: 43.8 g
- 18.9 grams of protein

Chicken Drumsticks with a Crusted Coating.

Time required for preparation: 10 minutes 4 portions (servings)

Ingredients:

- 1 pound boneless chicken drumsticks
- 1/2 cup buttermilk 1/2 cup panko breadcrumbs 1/2 cup sour cream

- 1/2 cup all-purpose flour 1/4 teaspoon baking powder

- Spice Mixture:

- 1/2 teaspoon of salt

- 1/2 teaspoon celery salt 1/4 teaspoon oregano

- 1/4 tsp. cayenne pepper 1 teaspoon of paprika

- 1/4 tsp. garlic powder (optional)

- 1/4 teaspoon dried thyme

- 1/2 tbsp. freshly grated ginger

- 1/2 tsp. freshly ground white pepper

- 1/2 tsp. Freshly ground black pepper, 3 tablespoons melted butter

Directions:

- Marinate the chicken in the buttermilk overnight in the refrigerator by covering it with plastic wrap. In a shallow baking dish, combine the spices with the flour, breadcrumbs, and baking powder.

- After removing the chicken from the milk, cover it well with the flour spice combination.

- Place the chicken drumsticks in the Ninja Oven's Air fryer basket and cook until golden brown.

- Pour the melted butter over the drumsticks and serve immediately.

- Selecting the "Air fry" mode is accomplished by turning the dial. Next, press the

Time button once more, and this duration turns the dial to set the cooking time to ten minutes.

- Now press the Temp button and turn the dial to 425 degrees Fahrenheit to complete the setting.

- Place the baking pan inside the oven after it has been warmed.

- Cook the drumsticks for another 10 minutes once they have been flipped.

- Warm the dish before serving.

Nutrition:

- Calories in a serving: 331

- 2.5 g of fat

- Carbohydrates: 69 g

- 28.7 grams of protein

Turkey Meatballs.

Preparation time: 20 minutes 6 individual servings

Ingredients:

- 1 pound of turkey, minced

- Deseeded and sliced 1 red bell pepper 1 red onion 1/4 cup mayonnaise 1 big egg, beaten 4 tbsp. Parsley (minced), 1 tbsp. cilantro (minced), season with salt to taste

- season with freshly ground black pepper to taste

Directions:

- Combine all the meatball ingredients in a large mixing bowl and combine. Small meatballs may be made from this mixture and placed in an air fryer basket to cook until done.

- To choose the "Air Fry" mode, press the "Power Button" on the Air Fry Oven and turn the dial to the right. To adjust the cooking time to 20 minutes, press the Time button twice and turn the dial one again.

- Now, press the "Temp" button and adjust the dial to the desired temperature of 375oF (degrees Fahrenheit). After warming the oven, insert the air fryer basket inside and close the lid. Warm the dish before serving.

Nutrition:

- calorie count: 338

- 9.7 g of fat

- Carbohydrates: 32.5 g

- Protein content: 10.3 g

Meatballs made with ground chicken.

Time required for preparation: 10 minutes 4 portions (servings)

Ingredients:

- 1 pound of ground chicken

- 13 cup panko bread crumbs 1 teaspoon of salt

- 2 tbsp. chopped chives

- 1/2 teaspoons garlic powder 1 teaspoon dried thyme

- 1 quail (egg)

Directions:

- Combine all the meatball ingredients in a large mixing bowl and combine. Small meatballs may be made from this mixture and placed in an air fryer basket to cook until done.

- To choose the "Air Fry" mode, press the "Power Button" on the Air Fry Oven and turn the dial to the right. To adjust the cooking time to 10 minutes, press the Time button twice and turn the dial one again.

- Now, press the "Temp" button and adjust the dial to the 350oF setting to complete the process. After warming the oven, insert the air fryer basket inside and close the lid. Warm the dish before serving.

Nutrition:

- Calories in a serving: 453

- 2.4 g of fat

- Carbohydrates: 18 g

- Protein content: 23.2 g

Chicken Meatballs with Parmesan Cheese.

Preparation time: 1/2 minutes 4 portions (servings)

Ingredients:

- 1 pound of ground chicken 1 big egg that has been beaten

- 1/2 cup finely grated Parmesan cheese

- 1/2 cup pork rinds, finely chopped Garlic powder (one teaspoon)

- 1 teaspoon of paprika

- 1 teaspoon of kosher salt

- 1/2 tsp. black pepper

- 1/2 cup ground pork rinds for the crust

Directions:

- Combine all the meatball ingredients in a large mixing bowl and combine. Small meatballs may be formed from this mixture and rolled in the pig rinds to finish them off.

- Place the meatballs in the air fryer basket once they have been coated. The "Bake" mode may be selected by pressing the "Power Button" on your Air Fry Oven and turning the dial.

- To adjust the cooking time to 1/2 minute, press the "Time" button twice more and spin the dial one more. Now, press the Temp button and adjust the dial to the 400oF setting to complete the process.

- After warming the oven, insert the air fryer basket inside and close the lid.

- Warm the dish before serving.

Nutrition:

- calorie count: 529

- 17 g of fat

- Carbohydrates: 55 g

- 41 g of protein

Italian Meatballs Made in Minutes.

Preparation time: 13 minutes 4 portions (servings)

Ingredients:

- 1/4 cup finely chopped onion 2 lbs. lean ground turkey

- 2 garlic cloves, minced 2 tablespoons parsley, chopped 2 eggs

- grated 1/1/2 cup parmesan cheese

- 1/1/2 teaspoon red pepper flakes

- 1/2 tsp. Italian seasoning (optional)

- Season with salt and freshly ground black pepper to taste

Directions:

- Combine all the meatball ingredients in a large mixing bowl and combine. Small meatballs may be made from this mixture and placed in an air fryer basket to cook until done.

- To choose the "Air Fry" mode, press the "Power Button" on the Air Fry Oven and turn the dial to the right. Next, select "Time" from the menu bar, then spin the dial to set the cooking time to 13 minutes. Now, press the Temp button and crank the dial to the 350oF setting on the oven.

- After warming the oven, insert the air fryer basket inside and close the lid.

- When the meatballs are half-cooked, turn them over and repeat the process.

- Warm the dish before serving.

Nutrition:

- Calories in a serving: 472

- Fat: 25.8 g Carbohydrates: 1.7 g

- Protein content: 59.6 g

Chicken Breast with Oregano.

Time required for preparation: 25 minutes, 6 individual servings

Ingredients:

- 2 lbs. boneless chicken breasts (minced). 1 tablespoon of avocado oil

- 1 teaspoon smoked paprika Garlic powder (one teaspoon)

- 1 teaspoon dried oregano

- 1/2 teaspoon of salt

- season with freshly ground black pepper to taste

Directions:

- Combine all the meatball ingredients in a large mixing bowl and combine. Small meatballs may be made from this mixture and placed in an air fryer basket to cook until done.

- To choose the "Air Fry" mode, press the "Power Button" on the Air Fry Oven and turn the dial to the right. Once again, press the "Duration" button and spin the dial to set the cooking time to 25 minutes. NOTE:

- By now, you should have the temperature set at 375 degrees Fahrenheit by pressing and rotating the Temp button.

- After warming the oven, insert the air fryer basket inside and close the lid.

- Warm the dish before serving.

Nutrition:

- calorie count: 352

- 1/4 g of fat

- Carbohydrates: 15.8 g

- 26 g of protein

Salmon with a Cajun twist.

Time required for preparation: 10 minutes

Ingredients: 2 salmon steaks (serves 2) Preparation:

- 2 tbsp. of the mixture

- seasoning with cajun seasoning

Directions:

- The Cajun seasoning should be applied evenly to the salmon steaks. Set the bowl aside for approximately 10 minutes. Place the salmon steaks on a prepared baking sheet and bake for 15 minutes.

- Place the drip pan at the bottom of the Instant Vortex Air Fryer Oven's cooking chamber to catch any drips. "Air fry" should be selected, and then the temperature should be set at 390°F. Set the timer for 8 minutes and hit the "Start" button.

- When the display indicates that "Add Food" should be done, place the cooking tray in the center of the oven. Flip the salmon steaks when the display indicates that the food should be turned.

- Removing the tray from the Vortex Oven after the cooking time has expired is a good idea. Serve when still heated.

Nutrition:

- 225 calories Carbohydrates: 0 g 10.5 grams of fat 22.1 g of protein

Buttered Salmon.

Time required for preparation: 10 minutes 2 portions (servings)

Ingredients:

- 2 salmon fillets (6 ounces each)

- Season with salt and freshly ground black pepper as needed. 1 tablespoon melted butter

Directions:

- Season each salmon fillet with salt and freshly ground black pepper before brushing it with melted butter. Arrange the salmon fillets on a baking sheet that has been buttered.

- Place the drip pan at the bottom of the Instant Vortex Air Fryer Oven's cooking chamber to catch any drips. Choosing "Air Fry" and adjusting the temperature to 360°F are the next steps. Set the timer for 10 minutes and hit the "Start" button.

- When the display indicates that "Add Food" should be done, place the cooking tray in the center of the oven. When the display indicates that the food should be turned, flip the salmon fillets.

- Removing the tray from the Vortex Oven after the cooking time has expired is a good idea. Serve when still heated.

Nutrition:

- 276 calories, 0 grams of carbohydrates, 16.3 grams of fat, 33.1 g of protein

Salmon with a lemony tang.

Time required for preparation: 10 minutes 2 portions (servings)

Ingredients:

- 1 tablespoon freshly squeezed lemon juice
- 1/2 tablespoon extra-virgin olive oil
- Season with salt and freshly ground black pepper as needed. 1 garlic clove, peeled and minced
- chopped1/2 tbsp. fresh thyme leaves (optional) (7oz.) Salmon fillets are a delicacy.

Directions:

- Combine all of the ingredients (except the salmon) in a large mixing bowl and combine. Add the salmon fillets and liberally cover them with the sauce mixture.
- Place the salmon fillets, skin-side down, on a lightly oiled baking sheet or rack. Place the drip pan at the bottom of the Instant Vortex Air Fryer

Oven's cooking chamber to catch any drips. Select "Air Fry" and raise the temperature to 400 degrees Fahrenheit. Set the timer for 10 minutes and hit the "Start" button.

- When the display indicates that "Add Food" should be done, place the cooking rack in the lowest position. When the display indicates that the food should be turned, turn the fillets.

- Removing the tray from the Vortex Oven after the cooking time has expired is a good idea. Serve when still heated.

Nutrition:

- Calories in 1 serving: 297 Carbohydrates: 0.8 g 15.8 g of fat 38.7 g of protein

Salmon with Miso Glaze.

Time required for preparation: 10 minutes 4 portions (servings)

Ingredients:

- 1 / 3 cup sake

- 1/4 cup sugar 1/4 cup miso (red miso)

- 1 tablespoon soy sauce (low sodium) 2 tablespoons of extra-virgin olive oil

- 4 salmon fillets (5 ounces each), skinless (1-inch thick)

Directions:

- Add the sake, sugar, miso, soy sauce, and oil in a mixing bowl and whisk until well blended. Using a liberal amount of the mixture, rub the salmon fillets. Place the salmon fillets and any residual miso mixture in a plastic zip-lock bag and seal the bag.

- Close the bag and place it in the refrigerator to marinate for approximately 30 minutes. Prepare a baking dish that will fit into the Vortex Air Fryer Oven by brushing it with cooking oil. Take the salmon fillets out of the bag and brush off any excess marinade accumulated. Place the salmon fillets in the baking dish that has been prepared.

- Place the drip pan at the bottom of the Instant Vortex Air Fryer Oven's cooking chamber to catch any drips. Choose "Broil" and set the timer for 5 minutes on the stove.

- When the display indicates that "Add Food" should be done, place the baking dish in the center of the oven.

- When the display indicates that the food should be turned, do not turn the food. Removing the baking dish from the Vortex Oven once the cooking time has expired is important. Serve when still heated.

Nutritional Information:

- 335 calories

- Carbohydrates: 18.3 g

- 16.6 g of fat

- 29.8 g of protein

Tilapia with a spicy sauce.

Preparation time: 1/2 minutes 2 portions (servings)

Ingredients:

- 1/2 tsp. seasoning with lemon pepper

- 1/2 tsp. garlic powder (optional)

- 1/2 teaspoons onion powder

- Season with salt and freshly ground black pepper as needed. 2 tilapia fillets (6 ounces each)

- 1 tablespoon extra-virgin olive oil

Directions:

- Combine the spices, salt, and black pepper in a small mixing bowl until well combined. Next, prepare the tilapia fillets by coating them with oil and then rubbing them with the spice mixture. Place the tilapia fillets, skin-side down, on a lightly oiled cooking rack and bake for 15 minutes.

- Place the drip pan at the bottom of the Instant Vortex Air Fryer Oven's cooking chamber to catch any drips. Choosing "Air Fry" and adjusting the temperature to 360°F are the next steps. Set the timer for 1/2 minute and hit the "Start" button.

- When the display indicates that "Add Food" should be done, place the cooking rack in the lowest position. When the display indicates that the food should be turned, turn the fillets.

- Removing the tray from the Vortex Oven after the cooking time has expired is a good idea. Serve when still heated.

Nutrition:

- Calories: 206 per serving Carbohydrates: 0.2 g 8.6 g of fat 31.9 g of protein

Conclusion

Foods that will be consumed at least three days after being prepared, such casseroles, may benefit greatly from being frozen. Frozen food is practical and safe to eat, but it can't always take the place of fresh ingredients in a recipe. As an illustration, the components for a slow-cooked dinner may also be pre-frozen and then added to the slow cooker, where they are left to boil during the cooking duration. This allows you to prepare meals up to two months in advance, saving you a significant amount of time and cutting down on the time required for meal preparation. The final factor of food safety that should be taken into account when preparing meal plans is how you will reheat your meals. You are welcome to use any other traditional heating device in your kitchen if you choose; nevertheless, the great majority of people choose to reheat their meals in the microwave.

On the other side, while using a microwave to prepare food, you must be extremely careful to avoid overcooking it because this might give the dish an undesirable texture and flavor. You may avoid this problem more easily if you prepare or defrost your meals in one-minute intervals. Instead of leaving the meat in large chunks before cooking, split it up into smaller pieces. By doing this, you can guarantee that the meat will cook through the dish more quickly and evenly. Anything taken out of the freezer and put right into the microwave should never be nuked. Verify that the frozen food has had enough time to defrost.

In addition to shrinking the size of your stomach, bariatric surgery also changes the path that food takes through your digestive system before reaching your intestines. As a result, following surgery, it's crucial to make sure you're getting enough nutrition while simultaneously lowering your total body mass. An air fryer is a useful kitchen appliance that might help you meet the low-fat dietary objectives of a bariatric eating plan. By using this culinary equipment, you can simply prepare scrumptious meals that are nutritional and safe for surgery patients.

The move to a healthy lifestyle that supports your weight loss objectives may take some time and work, but nothing is impossible if you carefully plan your meals and use adaptable kitchen appliances like an air fryer. Naturally, the primary determinant in deciding your long-term safety and success will be how frequently you have follow-up appointments with your surgeon and the rest of the surgical team. It is advised that you continue to get your teeth examined once a year after you have completed all of the appointments that were planned for the first year.

www.ingramcontent.com/pod-product-compliance
Lightning Source LLC
Chambersburg PA
CBHW071019050325
22997CB00026B/241